A
CALENDAR
OF
FESTIVALS

Marian Green has studied and worked with the
natural and folk traditions for many years. She
has been the editor of *Quest* quarterly magazine
since 1970 and runs courses and gives talks
throughout Britain, Europe and Canada.

A
CALENDAR
OF
FESTIVALS

Traditional Celebrations, Songs,
Seasonal Recipes & Things to Make

Marian Green

ELEMENT
Shaftesbury, Dorset ● Rockport, Massachusetts

© Marian Green 1991

Published in Great Britain in 1991 by
Element Books Limited
Longmead, Shaftesbury, Dorset

Published in the USA in 1991 by
Element, Inc
42 Broadway, Rockport, MA 01966

Cover illustration by Jackie Morris
Designed by Nancy Lawrence
Typeset by Burns and Smith Ltd., Derby
Printed and bound in Great Britain by
Billings Ltd, Hylton Road, Worcester

British Library Cataloguing in Publication Data

Green, Marian
A calendar of festivals: traditional celebrations, songs, seasonal recipes & things to make
I. Title
394.26
ISBN 1-85230-204-6

Library of Congress Data available

CONTENTS

Dedication

This book is dedicated to all those people, my friends past, present and future, who have the light of life in their eyes and the music in their heart because they have connected to the cycling seasons, and who hold the Earth as sacred. It is dedicated to all those who, even in the smallest degree, keep alive the old feasts, the ancient dances and the traditions of love and magic which make the world go round, and to their children, in the hope that they too will be able to dance to Mother Earth's heartbeat, and delight in her flowers and wildlife, in freedom, wherever on the globe they may be.

May the Blessing of Life shine on all.

Marian Green

Lady For All Seasons

I am the singing of ice in a frozen river;
I am the perfume of Spring in the first flowers;
I am the voice of the wind in the bare branches;
I am the patter of raindrops on unfurling petals;
I am rich nectar in the foaming white May flowers;
I am the joy of the bees among roses;
I am the warmth of moonlight on a still evening;
I am the scarlet of poppies in golden cornfields;
I am the peace after harvest, the essence of vineyards;
I am the bounty of orchards, the treasure of plenty;
I am the silence of woodsmoke from the fires of autumn;
I am the repose of all Nature and the star of Midwinter;
I am the cycle, continually turning.
All seasons see me with my faces of flowers,
But you have forgotten to honour the changes,
You have forgotten the power of transformation,
From birth into childhood, through love and compassion,
But I have not left you nor silenced my singing,
I will continue creating the seasons, for
I am the singing of ice in a frozen river...

Marian Green

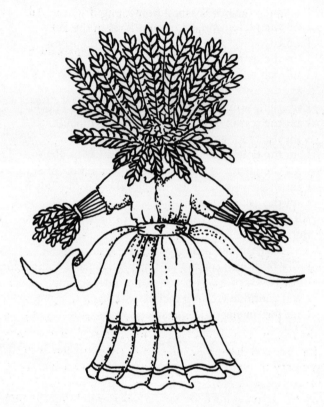

INTRODUCTION

Sing a song of Seasons! Something Bright in All!
Flowers in the Summer, Fires in the Fall.

Robert Louis Stevenson: '*Autumn Fires*'

The Bible says 'There is a Time for every purpose under heaven ...' but we have become dislocated from our natural roots, and no longer sense the rhythms and patterns of the Seasons. Modern living gives us light at the touch of a switch, strawberries at Christmas, and roses in February. We no longer watch from our rural window the sweep of green touching the brown fields as the days of March lengthen, nor do we watch the leaves of the lime trees, like verdant flames, consume each branch from the tip as the April sun draws the sap upwards. We no longer fear the first frost which burns the grass white, and turns the trees from green to flame and then to the charred darkness of barren winter, for we will have heat and comfort and food in plenty through the hungry gap, when nature sleeps. In some ways we are fortunate in seeming to be in control of the seasons, but we are now beginning to see at what cost this control was bought.

The end of the twentieth century has been a time of great change, in political and environmental fields. Things unthought of in the 1950s, the bright expansive days after the war, have become commonplace; worldwide communication via satellites, fifty channels of television programmes in colour, kiwi fruit with everything, the fall of the Berlin Wall and the vast changes within the Communist World. This wider vision of world affairs has also brought with it the reverse side of the coin – nuclear contamination and pollution which are no respecters of national boundaries; overuse of

chemicals destroying the life in the soil and in rivers; chemical spillages on land and sea harming all who live beneath the dark pall of human enterprise and greed. These negative factors are reasons why people are beginning to seek other ways of doing things.

We know that the Earth can heal herself, given *no* help from humanity and about seventy years of peace, as she has done after great volcanic eruptions, floods and hurricanes. Perhaps humanity is not essential to the evolution of the planet, although we see ourselves as crucial components in the chain of life. We are at a great turning point in our history; if we do nothing to prevent it, chemical changes in the atmosphere, the results of our own industrial emissions, will cause the sea levels to rise, and the protective ozone layer above us to decay, allowing harmful radiation to bring us more cancers, cataracts and death in other ways. We are heading towards our own suicide, unless we take action now by cutting back on energy use, abandoning the convenience of our own cars for the pollution-free bicycle, or even our ancestors' Shanks's pony.

In our desire to control nature and greed to plunder the earth, we have all but lost the harmony that should exist between humanity and the earth. Even now we are only just beginning to apprehend the spiritual cost of this divorce of the soul of the people from the spirit of the land. We are the poorer for this separation because we have had part of our inner heritage stolen from us. Once you lose step with the rhythm of Nature you are lost, because without a great effort you cannot catch up. Being out of step has led to dislocations, a feeling of detachment and alienation, because the roots our families used to have in a place and a landscape have been torn away or allowed to wither because we didn't know that they mattered. This may well be the underlying cause of many of the illnesses we suffer, the ennui, the boredom with artificial amusements, the anxieties we feel about something too nebulous to identify. We have lost touch with our Native Land, become orphaned of our Mother Earth.

If we can make ourselves aware of the real importance of being in touch with Nature, of connecting and rerooting ourselves into the rhythms of the Earth, we immediately gain a stability and a firm base. If we are willing to recognise the festive cycle of an orthodox faith, or the stronger links between the World and her children, found or rediscovered in alternative religions, and come to know how sacred the seasons are, we will take steps towards becoming whole. Wholeness and Holiness are linked in their meanings. If we restore our scattered selves to wholeness we will experience the holiness of many of the things about us.

Sadly, there are very few manmade things which are holy of themselves. Cathedrals, churches, chapels, and the priests who minister therein have had holiness poured upon them from one who has, himself, been so annointed. In earlier times things and places were holy because it was their nature to be healing, that is making whole, or holy. We each have a spark of the divine life force within us, yet that cries out with a quiet voice unheard in the modern world. Once you are willing to learn to let that heart-spark experience the joy of a shared religious or seasonal festival, seeing it anew as a genuine and valuable link with our earthly heritage, you cannot but gain.

Unless the population is vastly reduced in the consumer-led lands of the Western World, it is not likely that we will return to simple village life, self-sufficient yet guided by the turn of the seasons as to what we eat and what tasks we have to do. We have become too used, anyway, to the comforts of modern living and would find it hard to cope with crop rotation and animal husbandry. We have largely become Urban Souls who feel alienated from our Mother Earth and intimidated by the agricultural activities of our country brethren. The way ahead does not lead backwards into some imaginary idyllic rural lifestyle, but forwards towards a new partnership and spiritual awareness of what Nature can offer. We must restore our links with the cogwheels of the seasons; learn to flow, and welcome the healing that this can bring to the frazzled nerves, the anxious mind and the denatured soul.

In times past the country folk, who made up the largest part of our population, were forced to live their lives in harmony with the seasons, dependent on the weather, the winds, the needs of livestock and the unchanging pattern of the agricultural round: sowing, weeding, reaping, threshing and so on. This well established rhythm was more or less the same from the Bronze Age until the Industrial Revolution, when transport and industries tore many country folk from their roots, built cities around them and began the great rift between the People and the Earth.

But despite the great changes, a strong traditional rhythm of celebrations, fêtes, fairs and ancient festivals remained, keeping time with an older drum: the heartbeat of Mother Nature underlying everything. We still catch faint echoes of this primal rhythm in the Church's Calendar of Feast Days and Holy Days, in rural traditions and country customs, dating back to time immemorial. In some places, old dances and celebrations are being revived in an unstoppable surge of some arcane energy, or perhaps the simple desire to make a few pounds from tourists; often both these impulses are intertwined.

Newcomers to villages are seeking to unite in spirit with the farm labourers they have displaced and are genuinely trying to revive local Well Dressing Ceremonies, Ox Roasts and Country Fairs. Their children are learning to dance around the replaced Maypole on the village green and go 'Trick or Treating' at Hallowe'en (a custom old in Britain long before it went westwards to America, and more recently rebounded to its native shores). Morris Dancers reinvoke their magic with bells and music, with leaps and clashing sticks, recalling ancient times.

Traditional dishes are being rediscovered to deck the board in country pubs and up-market restaurants: naturally produced meat; organic vegetables with their almost forgotten taste and texture; farm cheeses; and locally caught, smoked fish. All these remnants from the past are being recovered, dusted off and shown again to appreciative customers all over the country.

These things are not all fake, not all amusements to entertain the newcomer country dwellers, or to bring visitors in to clutter the village shop and pack the 'Rose and Crown' to overflowing. There is a deep, underlying current which draws people back towards their rural heritage, to reconnect their modern, urban selves to some simpler, more natural foundation from which they have become detached. Now, having most things in the material world, they begin to discover this loss of balancing connection to the Earth.

This discovery is taking a number of different directions. In some it is a move towards Green Politics, urging care of the environment both at home and abroad; in others it is a spiritual quest, for that Holy Grail of self-assurance and inner peace. Some strive to reawaken old ways of living, traditional crafts, forgotten skills and customs, dances and celebrations, drawing to them others who have felt a similar unconscious loss. It is not simply a matter of yearning for some rustic past, but a genuine, soul-deep longing for something which modern life does not provide. Not even the churches can provide this spiritual nourishment. It is something deeper that is craved, something purer, closer to the source of the Spring of Inspiration, perhaps, or to the original Rhythm of Life itself.

Revivals of Traditional Festivals and Dances, the sacred bonfire parties, the seasonal gathering on a hill top or beside the village pump, the processions from the Christian churches often carrying pagan symbols, or performing pre-Christian rites, awakens a dim echo in many people which is more than just the impulse to take part in a colourful or folksy spectacle. There is in people a deep-seated desire to acknowledge the passing of the seasons, the times and tides which wait for no-one, and to rebuild, perhaps on grafted roots, a heartfelt link with Tradition and the Old Ways. The seasons are sacred because the Earth, our much neglected and mistreated Mother, is sacred. The patterns of old feasts and celebrations mark the unity of mankind and planet, attuning both to a natural harmony, which in its turn will bring peace and plenty from the life of the land.

This book tries to rediscover ancient meanings in celebrations which still persist today in remote villages and in city centres after many hundreds, or perhaps thousands, of years. These celebrations bring together people whose ancestors have dwelt in that place for centuries with those incoming folk whose inner longing is to reconnect to natural foundations, to share the same ritual, procession or act of worship or thanksgiving that others have done, upon that spot, for generations. Within the cycle of the seasons are those markstones in the life of an individual, celebrated by church or family, yet in turn linking the one person with the land as a whole. The Birth of the Christ Child at Christmas recalls the birth of any child, bringing joy to his family; the Rites of Passage through Naming, Betrothal, Marriage, Retirement, Death and perhaps to some, Rebirth in the Age to Come, reflect the passing seasons of Spring, Summer, Harvest, Autumn and Winter and the life renewed with the returning sun. In earlier times it was the pattern of the growth of foliage, the passing orb of Sun and Moon and the ebb and flow of the natural world which separated season from season, and their passing was marked with worship, celebration or lament as the cycles of the Earth unrolled.

The Older Gods and Goddesses lived their magical lives in the myths and tales of the people, retold around the winter fires or in the harvest fields, enacting parts of the Great Mystery Play of Life upon the worldly stage as every act, in its own hour, unfolded. Many of those old tales persist, and the dances and the mimes, the peculiar traditions and half-forgotten arts are being reawoken to meet a modern need. A new pagan spirit which, above all other things, holds the Earth herself as sacred is being revealed to those who choose to look. The name Gaia is voiced abroad; Goddess of the globe of Earth, a living, sentient being, now so scarred and poisoned by our careless greed, is being spoken to with reverence. We need to relearn to dance with her cyclic rhythms.

To ancient people the Earth was sacred and their temples were natural places where old power was felt – free-running springs, white rocks, old trees and hidden caves. There, pledges were made, or healing sought, or acts of worship, marriage or requiem were shared. Some of the power still lingers and those of us with moon-filled eyes have seen it, felt its peaceful rush, or have sought communion with the natural flow, hoping for strength or aid or quiet content.

Such basic resources can be beyond price in an ever-more hectic world. We need the respite of being able to walk in high places, breathe the scents of wild flowers and unpolluted air, for here it becomes natural to worship the Creator, and honour the Earth, from whose bones and beasts and plants our own bodies are created. By rediscovering the pattern of changing seasons, celebrating the festivals, understanding the links with an ancient past and a heritage of harmony with the flowers of each month we regain understanding of our kinship with Nature, and the essential strength such kinship brings.

In each chapter I have tried to uncover just a few of the many local or widespread festivities, to show the changing flowers of field and garden and reveal how the often imperceptible changes on the face of Nature bring about corresponding changes in our own lives. At best this can only be a sampler, a taster of the rich variety of regional and seasonal activities, the special dishes, the processions and children's dances which demonstrate so clearly the enduring bonds of the people's lives with the land beneath their feet.

The forces of Life, so often depicted as Jack in the Green, and the pagan Goddesses associated with the Earth, Moon and sea still watch over us from house beam and church roof, from cottage lintel and the carved façades of municiple buildings all over the land. The spirit of ever-changing vitality and growth has always been with us, but we have overlooked these all-seeing presences in our electrically lit, centrally heated and totally controlled urban existences. Now it is time to pause and look at the roots of things, and sense with heart rather than intellect the old connection with the Earth; for we are her children, born of her matter, living on her mantle, and she, once revered as holy, now needs care and protection from her unfeeling brood.

FEBRUARY

February fill the dyke, Be it black or be it white,
But if 'tis white 'tis better to like.

Country saying

Why begin with February? This book looks at the calendar of natural feasts, traditional happenings and local customs based on mankind's timescale in correlation with the seasons, rather than with the modern, artificial timetable. It is one of the things we have exchanged for the clockwork tick of our modern lives. It is a sad loss, giving a feeling of being out of step with the real world. By recognising that Mother Nature has a calendar all of her own, whose ever moving sundial marks the hours of passing time with shadows, with the flush of new green growth across the meadows, and by gilding the forest trees with autumn, we can realign ourselves with Earth time. The first days of February are when Spring's alarm clock chimes and with each drip of melting ice, awakens all the land. The very first flowers of that natural year, the snowdrops, harbingers of warmth to come, raise up their white and green petalled bells, reminding us that summer will return.

In today's world we have largely forgotten that we are part of Nature. We take our timing from clocks and calendars, fixed by man-made timetables, and through the wonders of modern technology ignore the rising and setting of the sun, the passing of the seasons in their own season, when the flowering or fruiting of trees gave a regular, but shifting pattern to the tasks of the people. To overlook this link with Nature is foolish, for it dislocates us from the very roots of our being. Today we seem to have no need for Maypole Dancing nor Well Dressing except as a sort of spiritual tourist attraction – or do we? Those who participate in the old, traditional calendar customs nearly all report feelings of life, of joy and of unleashed tension and renewal. These links between us as earthly beings and the Earth as Mother Nature have a deep-seated influence over our feelings of security and cyclic change. Once that connection is broken we drift, anchorless in the sea of confusion, somehow sensing a loss we cannot understand or define. Those who have taken up the Old Faith, or sought comfort and stability in the reawakening of ancient customs, have somehow healed that rift within.

February is the month when Mother Nature restores herself, and it is a good time, when the first green stirrings of growing life appear, to think hard about our own connections with the Earth. It is an opportunity to remake those inner links with self and season, allowing the calendar customs to join us with the Earth beneath our feet, which physically and spiritually sustains us.

All we need to do is to become aware of the passing moons, the dates which our ancestors held as sacred, the patterns of living which Nature uses to restore the natural world. We too can be healed, balanced and gain security, if we are willing to acknowledge the joy of spring, the delights of summer, the repose of autumn and the deep rest of silent winter.

We are also approaching the Age of Aquarius which will replace the regimentation of the Great Sign of Pisces which has held sway for about two thousand years. Most of the month of February falls within the Sign of Aquarius, which is the zodiac sign of the New Age. It will be a time of great change, as is each annual spring, when the dead of winter slowly awakens to the light of spring. When the world enters the Sign of Aquarius there will be a great awakening to a new light, and a new awareness of a brighter dawn. We need to learn again this connection with the turning Earth so that Nature's Laws and Nature's own timetable can help our individual cog to refit into the Wheel of Life. Once you begin to sense this old calendar of change, of flowering, fruiting, seeding and repose within your own life, you will gain an inner stability and from that, strength. Sense February as a new beginning to your own pattern and many things will start to fall into place, and understanding of your human nature as part of Nature may bring you comfort in the twilight before the growing season.

For all that, February can feel an uncomfortable month, dark and dreary after the bright lights of Christmas and the fervour of the New Year celebrations. In earlier times it was called 'the hungry gap', for little was left in the larder and the first new vegetables, fresh milk or unsalted meat were months away. In some circles it is known as the 'Cleansing Tide', the quarter of the solar year between Mid-Winter and the Spring Equinox, when the face of Nature is washed clean with snow and rain and the industrious housekeeper begins Spring Cleaning. Somehow, at this nadir time of year, it is easy to fall prey to depression or sadness, and often friendships end and deaths of distant relatives are brought to our attention with more than average frequency. It is a dark and gloomy month; this was felt by our ancestors, who, taking comfort from the first flowers they saw making headway through the melting snow, celebrated the feast of Brigit or Bride, later attributed to St Brigid. In the church it is called 'Candlemas'.

The Feast of Brigid

Brigid is an ancient Goddess associated with springs of water, with healing and childbirth, and for this reason she became the Midwife in the Christian story of the Nativity of Jesus. In her earlier form she was worshipped in Ireland by the setting out of the 'Bride's Bed', near to the hearth, which acted as the sacred centre of the firelit home. The Bride, a large Corn Sheaf, was decked with ribbons and bright pieces of cloth by the women of the family and set beside the fireplace. If any were found, the first shy snowdrops or early violets, or later, bright golden or purple crocuses, were placed about the house, alongside swathes of dark green ivy leaves. Each of the women poured a libation of milk or water with honey in it and made a wish. Later on, the menfolk were summoned, ribbons or greenery were wound about their heads and arms, and after they had paid a small fee, a coin, a flower posy or even a kiss to the Lady of the house, they too could enter the circle of firelight and ask for help with their work, the craft or trade they would be following throughout the coming year.

In some places all the household candles were blessed, for it was felt that already the days had grown that little bit longer than the midwinter dark and that candles need not be used so much. In modern versions of this old celebration, many small candles are placed in trays around the room and briefly lit, bringing a great blaze of flame light to the winter evening. Later they are snuffed and used as votive candles or for meditation during the rest of the year. Churches, too, bless their candles on this feast, and reckon it was the day when the Virgin Mary was cleansed after the birth of Jesus, and took him to the Temple, where it was prophesied that he would be a 'Light to the world'.

Mother Nature is seen as being renewed at this time; she becomes the Maiden of Spring, when the lambs' tails of hazel catkins tremble on the bare branches, and the hardiest of bulbs begin their new lease of life, thrusting green spears through the thawing mould. New life is born too, for the first lambs are born in sheltered pastures, giving the Celtic name to this early part of February – *Oimelc*, 'Ewes' milk'. Rather than being the rare, healthfood milk that it is today, it was a vital part of the family's nourishment in this starved time of year. The gambolling lambs seemed to herald the warmer days to come, and

overhead, the harbingers of spring, the overwintering birds, were beginning to verbally stake their claims on their territory and sing a song of mating as the weeks of February passed by.

Valentine's Day

The mating songs bring reminders of a more widely known February custom, the sending of Valentine Cards or gifts. Like many old customs, its roots are lost but there are several traditions concerning the formation of loving bonds at this time of the year. Geoffrey Chaucer wrote about the birds mating for life at this season in his 'Parliament of the Fowles', but he may be recalling an earlier Roman feast, the 'Festival of Faunus', the Latin equivalent of Pan, the Greek God of Wildlife. Many old country celebrations were held during this month, when birds were building their nests and billing and cooing in every tree and garden.

There were at least two 'Saint Valentines' who were martyred. One of them was supposed to have left a last message to his lady love, scratched on the wall of his condemned cell, signed 'Your Valentine'; and from this the whole ongoing idea of sending poems, messages or cards has grown up.

In some places, in order to bring young people together, a game was played in which everyone's name was written on a scrap of paper, and the girls each drew a boy's name, and the boys a girl's name, and each would search out their partners, two each, from whom to choose a lover. In Victorian times printed cards started to be sent anonymously, as well as the more personal handmade verses and pictures, or pressed flowers which expressed very specific emotions from mild flirtation to undying passion. Some of these nineteenth-century cards are now collectors' items. Today, commercial interests dominate and the verses inside the cards are often rude or not so kind – 'Pimples are red, bruises are blue, If you come near me, I'll give these to you!' Not a heart or flower in sight.

Watery Customs

Because water is important at this time of year, several of the local calendar customs include a kind of well dressing or blessing, and several of the 'Football' types of games use streams as part of the playing field or goal posts. At the start of February, at St Ives in Cornwall, they hold a festival combining several traditions. Part of the festival involves the dressing of St Ea's well with ivy leaves and any early flowers, especially snowdrops, winter-flowering jasmine and even very early daffodils, if any have appeared in Cornwall's balmy winter weather. This fresh water spring, quite close to the beach, is surrounded by a granite frontage and is supposed to mark the spot where St Ea arrived after drifting across from Ireland on an ivy leaf. The well runs even in very dry summers and has the reputation of healing eye complaints and poor sight, if the water is ritually splashed on them three times. The well is blessed by the local vicar, and often there is music, guising (dressing up in a variety of costumes and masks, from the root of 'disguise')

and a procession to the church yard where another ancient tradition is enacted. Here a silver ball is tossed against the church wall and when it falls among the gathered people it is carried off, usually by the younger villagers. As the church clock starts to strike twelve whoever has the ball is rewarded with a small money prize. Sometimes new pennies which have been heated up are thrown for the children to catch from the balcony of the Town Hall. Both the shiny silver ball and the bright, hot new pennies represent ancient symbols of the Sun whose power is being reawakened to bring about the warmer days of spring.

Football is a popular game, played by boys and men of all ages, as well as some girls too. Not all the games were played on neat grassy pitches, however: going back through history, at about the beginning of the Christian season of Lent, there were often wild ball games, involving kicking or carrying a ball, barrel or 'bottle' into a goal at one end of a playing area up to two miles long. At Atherstone in Warwickshire, Shrove Tuesday afternoon is given over to an ancient game in the main street, when a large ball, filled with water to prevent it from being kicked too far, is scrambled for. The winners are the side which has the ball as the time of play ends at 5pm.

At Sedgefield, in County Durham, the goals

are both watery, one being a pond and the other a stream, and at Ashbourne in Derbyshire (a name associated with Spa Water) the Henmore stream seems to form much of the pitch for their local version, played on both Shrove Tuesday and Ash Wednesday. These games often have hundreds of participants, and in some towns and villages this old country sport has been forbidden and the crowded streets no longer surge with rival parishioners, or 'Uppies' and 'Doonies' vying for possession or scoring moves with a soggy ball in the wintery sunlight of February afternoons. Similar sports occur later in the year; at Kirkwall in Orkney it is part of the Christmas Day festivities.

Shrove Tuesday

Because the Christian festival of Easter is still fixed by the phases of the moon, it shifts about by almost a month, and this gives rise to the variation of all the ancient celebration dates within the forty days of Lent which precede Easter. Shrove Tuesday was so named because it was the day on which pious Christians received absolution and penance for their sins, having made confession or 'shrived' themselves. It was the beginning of the Lenten Fast of forty days without meat or delicacies such as eggs, honey or even fat; so these precious commodities were used up, cooked together in a pan making a pancake. The medieval pancake was a good deal more substantial than today's paper thin circle of golden batter; it may have contained dried fruit, spices and other sorts of rich or tasty food. As it was, February and March were hungry times when all that might be left for daily consumption would be rough bread, hard cheese and salty bacon, for very little would have survived in storage during the winter and nothing green to eat would yet be showing itself in the fields. In these times, a rich, spicy pancake would be a rare treat.

In an increasing number of villages, pancake races are being revived. The pancake is thrown and caught again as the pancake-tosser runs along the village street in an age-old race. The golden pancakes, like the shiny pennies or the silver ball,

represent the sun, rising and falling in the sky. They are another ancient form of prayer or invocation to the warmth of the sun to return and banish the bitter cold of winter. Olney in Buckinghamshire has a historic race in which residents of the town, dressed in cap and apron and holding their pans and pancakes, compete against each other. They have to toss the pancakes three times as they complete a course of nearly a quarter of a mile. Other such races are held in London, Bodiam in Sussex, Ely in Cambridgeshire and in Liverpool, as well as in many smaller places, often as part of some charity fundraising occasion. At Westminster School in London, a cook tosses a pancake over a high beam and representatives of each form, in fancy dress nowadays, scramble to catch and hang on to the major portion of the pancake, before it hits the ground, in order to win a small money prize.

Nature Stirs

If the soil is dry enough and not frozen, gardeners will be doing their best to get seeds into the ground, especially herbs to add flavour to the summer salads in the days to come. On the days after the New Moon in February it was traditional to sow rosemary, borage, coriander, marjoram and sorrel. The proper time for sowing can be judged to have arrived when the waterside alder trees and bushes begin to show their dark catkins.

Now begin the tasks of Lent, named from the Anglo-Saxon word 'lenctene' from which we get 'length', as the days indeed begin to lengthen. As the month passes more wild flowers can be seen; in sheltered places the yellow brushes of coltsfoot, used in herbal medicine against coughs and chest problems, and in warmer places, the first shy violets. Winter aconite and winter heliotrope are found in favourable conditions. As climatic changes seem to be already taking effect in England, many of the later and more tender flowers are showing themselves early. Our ancestors' flowery calendar is running fast, and the wild expectancy of the first blossoms of Spring is falling further back.

By the end of this short but often gloomy

month every tree and garden will be alive with the cheeping and fluttering of the courting and nesting pairs of birds, and some like the fairly rare Raven will already be sitting on eggs or feeding extremely early young, taking advantage of carrion caused by frosty nights. In the old days at the end of February the woods would be ringing with the sound of axes as trees were coppiced so that new shoots could provide building materials, wattles for fences and a stock of branches to feed the fire in due course. Now that more land is being planted with trees perhaps this useful craft will be revived over a wider area, and the pole lathes of 'bodgers' in the woods will be humming to turn out the rounded parts for table and chair legs, and other traditional commodities in the ancient way.

The Green Man

One face which turns up time and time again at traditional festivals as a mask, a dancer, a symbol of life peering down from the stonework of a church roof or municipal edifice is that of the Green Man. Foliate faces, both male and female, are found in churches and on buildings from Ireland to Iran. All through the middle ages masons, decorating the corbels, the roof bosses, and the choir stalls, the pinnacles and the water spouts, the fonts and the pulpits of churches all over Europe chose the Foliate Face, the God of Green Growth, or Sylvanus as their image. These sacred heads have no obvious place in Christianity. Nowhere are there Bible Stories of prophets or preachers who are part man and part plant, but within the older pagan world the Green God of Nature has a clear and enduring position.

He has been overlooked within the orthodox church wherein his face watches the congregations, he has even been largely overlooked by the neo-pagans, who prefer to exalt the Goddess images and power, yet there among the rafters of country chapel and city cathedral, he gazes down to this day. His is a powerful image. A face bearded with leaves, fruits, fronds; vines and flowers springing from his lips, curling in his hair,

entwining his limbs. He is clearly a symbol of growth after winter, new life after old, renewal and rebirth.

Leap Year

The last day of February has, in each fourth or 'leap' year, another connection with partnerships, for traditionally it is this rare date on which women may accost their chosen menfolk and propose marriage. The 'Leap Day' is added every four years to bring the solar year of 365¼ days into line with the calendar year of 365 days. In Scotland it is thought to be unlucky to be born on a Leap Year's Day. This is obviously true if you only get gifts or a party every fourth year! Traditionally it is attributed to Job as his birthday, as he had so much hard luck that even missing three out of four birthdays was his lot, especially as he 'cursed the day he was born.'

If a woman should decide to propose to her chosen love and he is foolish enough to refuse her, she would expect a valuable gift to be presented to her before Easter. In earlier times this was often a pair of gloves.

St Blaise

There are of course many other saints' days during this month, celebrated with greater or lesser formality, one of which is St Blaise's festival, held on 3 February, the earliest date on which Shrove Tuesday might fall. This Armenian martyr was famed for curing a lad who was choking on a fish bone; he thus became the patron saint of throats. In some churches, those with similar complaints seek blessing on this day from a priest who holds long, lighted candles crossed beneath the supplicant's chin. In an older context, Blaise was the teacher of the magician Merlin, healer and guide to King Arthur. The lighted candles of his festival remind us of Candlemas, when light returned and the days of Spring could be celebrated, no matter how tentative a hold she had upon the waking Earth.

AQUARIUS, THE WATER BEARER

The astrological sign which covers most of February is Aquarius, the Water Bearer. People whose birthdays fall between about 21 January and 20 February (this may vary a day or two in either direction, because astrologically it is when the Sun rises against the stars of the constellation Aquarius, which may change from year to year) will consider themselves to be Aquarians when they come to look at their horoscopes in the paper.

If your birthday falls within the first or last week or so of each sign, you will also have some of the characteristics of the previous or next sign. The basic influences do not switch immediately the signs change; there is a period, the Cusp, where astrological signs overlap. There is no such thing as a 'typical Aquarian', because everyone is different and will show the influence of the positions of the Moon and the other planets within the patterns of their natal chart.

Aquarians, whose sign is ruled by the influences of the planets Saturn and Uranus, show a suitably varied character. They are forward-looking and have interests in anything new, interests which are well-fed these days, with developments in computer technology and electronics, practical gadgets and useful new tools. They are practical and like to discover how things work by experimentation, rather than simply being told. Because this is an Air sign (all signs of the zodiac are associated with either Earth, Water, Fire or Air) it concerns the mind and intellect, which is often the ruling factor in Aquarians' lives, rather than the heart and emotions which may dominate some of the Water signs.

Aquarians are friendly and generally good judges of character, but sensitive to people's feelings, often wishing to help. Because Saturn is the 'Old Man' of the planets they value tradition, yet still seek new things and ideas. They may have quick wits or tempers caused by the explosive nature of the planet Uranus. Some can be moody and badly affected by the unkind words of others, holding deep feelings of hurt long after the speaker has forgotten his original reproof. Aquarians tend to be individualistic and quite happy to work on their own; they will enjoy the company of others but within a club or study class rather than as personal friends. Some can be rebellious or cranky, tactless or outspoken, especially if they have just discovered something which they consider important or revolutionary.

Aquarians are usually fairly healthy though not fitness freaks, but can suffer circulatory problems, cold feet, and occasionally trouble with their ankles.

They always want to improve things, including their own knowledge about the world. Charles Darwin was an Aquarian, so was Thomas Edison and, on the artistic front, the composers Mozart, Mendelssohn and Schubert, and the poets Lord Byron and Robbie Burns, represent some of the famous names of the sign.

Each sign of the zodiac has its connections with flowers and particular gem stones, which are supposed to influence the health or luck of their wearers. The flowers closely associated with Aquarius include the snowdrop, fox-gloves and gorse, whose almost perpetual flowering through the year, though especially important at this month of loving partnerships, has given rise to the saying: 'When Gorse is out of flower, kissing is out of season.' The gems and semi-precious stones include dark red garnets, white zircons, green malachite and black jet or onyx, and the metal used in jewellery for Aquarians is often platinum.

February Recipes

Baked Salmon

1 whole salmon (about 4 lbs/2kg) or a
   salmon steak for each person
4 oz/125g/½ cup butter
pinch of dried rosemary
grated nutmeg
salt and pepper
a few cloves
1 tsp vinegar
1 tsp lemon juice

Clean the fish. Rub it inside and out with the mixed seasonings. Grease a large oven-proof dish and place the fish in it. Cover with dots of butter and roast in a 350°F/180°C/Mark 4 oven for 20 minutes per pound, 40 minutes per kilogram, basting frequently.

   Serve the salmon on a warmed dish with wedges of lemon.

Festival Biscuits

These biscuits are excellent served at any festival, and the shapes they are made in can reflect seasonal changes – heart shapes for St Valentine; leaves and flowers for a Spring festival; candles and stars for Christmas; moons, suns and faces all the year round. If you make a small hole in the top of each shape before it is baked, it may be hung from a branch or Christmas tree, as is appropriate.

1 lb/500g/4 cups self-raising flour
½ tsp each ground ginger, mixed spices and
   cinnamon
6 oz/175g/¾ cup butter or margarine
1 tbsp chopped roasted nuts, preferably
   hazelnuts
3 level tbsp clear honey (melted in a bowl
   set over warm water)

Sieve together the flour and the spices, and rub in the fat. Add the nuts and the melted honey, and knead the mixture to make a firm dough.

Roll this out thinly on a floured board and cut out your chosen shapes. Place the biscuits on a greased baking tray and cook in a preheated 300°F/150°C/Mark 2 oven for 20 to 25 minutes, until the biscuits are golden brown. Cool them on a wire tray and then decorate as you like with coloured icing or melted chocolate. These will store in an airtight tin for a week or so, or they can be frozen.

Oimelc Sweet

Oimelc is the Celtic word for Ewe's milk, which used to be a common drink in earlier times. It became available after the birth of lambs in February. To celebrate the Festival of St Brigid, a dish of ewes' milk yogurt can be mixed with honey and crushed, toasted hazelnuts; all these foods are traditionally part of the Candlemas feast.

Pancakes

8 oz/250g plain flour
½ pint/30cl milk
1 egg
pinch of salt

Sift the flour and add the salt. Beat in the egg, then gradually add the milk, beating until smooth. Leave to stand for about one hour. Heat a little oil in a frying pan and, when very hot, pour in just enough batter to cover the bottom of the pan. Cook over a high heat until golden brown, then toss and cook the other side.

   Everyone has their own favourite pancake fillings, but for a rich pancake treat make a stack of pancakes using a half milk/half cream pancake mix. Sandwich the pancakes together using jam and cream and serve dredged with icing sugar.

A Valentine Basket to Make

This woven heart-shaped basket is simple to make, and it can be filled with small presents or flowers, to give to your loved one on Valentine's Day. For other occasions, such as Christmas or New Year, the colours may be gold and silver or red and green, instead of the Valentine white and red. Filled with sweets they make delightful gifts to hang on the Christmas Tree.

Take two pieces of different coloured construction paper or thin card, about 8 inches (20 centimetres) by 2½ inches (6 centimetres), fold them in half across the long side, round the outer end, and cut two equally spaced slits upwards from the fold. (Fig. 1). Make sure that the length of the cut is slightly longer than the width of the folded card.

Holding the two pieces at right angles (Fig. 2) pass strip A inside the fold of strip 1, then thread strip 2 through A, and finally let the fold of A rest inside strip 3. Then take strip B, push the fold of strip 1 through it, weave it over strip 2, and through strip 3. Complete the weaving with strip C, which is woven the same way as strip A. (Fig. 3). This will result in a chequered pattern of red and white, or whichever other contrasting colours you are using, and because the folds were interwoven, the basket should open out.

To complete the basket a strip of card or bright ribbon to form a handle needs to be stuck inside each 'v' of the heart. This will hold the basket firmly together. (Fig. 4)

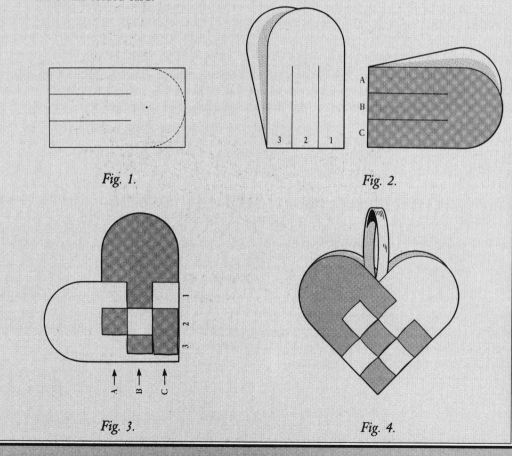

Fig. 1.

Fig. 2.

Fig. 3.

Fig. 4.

MARCH

Daffodils, that come before the swallow dares
and takes the winds of March with beauty:
Violets dim but sweeter than the lids of Juno's
eyes, Or Cytherea's breath; pale primroses, bold
oxlips ... and the crown imperial ....
W. Shakespeare: *The Winter's Tale*

March is a month of promises, of longer days drawing away from the gloom which always seems to descend after the bright lights of Christmas and the frenzy of the New Year celebrations. A soft green mist may be discerned across the brown fields sown with winter wheat, and if the weather has been especially favourable, both hedges and their banks are scattered with new emeralds from Spring's own verdant gown. Among these are the first wild jewels, golden shining celandines, and blue periwinkles peeping beneath their darker greenery. In gardens, bursts of early daffodils, narcissi and crocuses blaze in yellows and white among their spear-like, protective leaves. All around is the promise of the renewal of life after winter's sleep.

March traditionally is a month of varied winds, predicted by the saying 'March comes in like a lion and will go out like a lamb!' or, occasionally, the other way round. Wind was quite important to the old farmers, for it would dry and break up the topsoil, making the vital sowing of corn possible, and help to broadcast the seed in the traditional manner. A few weeks of dry weather would benefit the crop through its entire growth, and would speed up the greening of the meadows with new grass. In some parts of the country the countrymen would go out into a field and take off their trousers to sit with their bare buttocks on the earth to see if it felt warm enough for sowing the precious seed.

Saints' Days

The First of March is the feast of 'Dewi Sant', Wales' Saint David, when the Welsh Guards are presented with symbolic leeks to wear, and loyal Welsh folk the world over show the rather sweeter daffodil. The leek seems to have been adopted as a Welsh emblem because it is white and green, the colours of that nation's flag, which is now emblazoned with the Red Dragon as well. March the Second is dedicated to a more obscure saint, Chad, and its usually windy weather is foretold in a little verse,

> First comes David,
> Then comes Chad,
> Then comes Winnold,
> Roaring like mad!

St Winnold is a Breton saint celebrated in Cornwall, a land revelling in saints like a horse meadow revels in mushrooms, and many with as mysterious beginnings, too.

March Hares

At this time of year the hares are to be seen sparring for partners in the open fields. There are many strange tales about these beautiful, native creatures, whose presence in Britain long outdates rabbits which were introduced some say by the Romans, and others by the Normans, as delicacies for the Lords' tables. Hares were sacred to the Moon Goddess in many cultures, for they are frequently seen in the Spring dusk leaping and boxing against the rising full moon. Some medieval writers believed that hares were male one year and female the next, perhaps suggested by the fact that it is often the dominant females who are seen sparring for suitable males. Hare is seldom eaten as a meat in England, except as a kind of ritual dish, often jugged, cooked in its own blood. Horses share a similar sacredness, again being thought of as beasts associated with the mystical powers of the Moon, and their flesh has never been eaten here.

Hares are also associated with witches, for it was thought that these wise women could shapeshift into the form of hares in order to be out at night to attend their meetings on lonely moors and in secluded glades. Fisherfolk were wary of these charming creatures, and the sight of a hare when you were about to go to sea (or set off on a journey of any kind) was supposed to bring bad luck. If you did see one it was necessary, as on observing any other ill omen (such as a single magpie, or on discovering your jumper was on inside out or back to front) to return home, sit down, and then recommence the journey under hopefully more auspicious circumstances.

Rabbits, too, acquired some of the hare's mystique, and together with not encouraging women to set foot on a fishing boat, nor allowing them to whistle (especially near fishing gear, as they were thought to be able to summon unquiet winds), fishermen enlarged their list of superstitions to include mentioning rabbits or bringing one onto a boat. Anyone who broke this rule had to perform an elaborate penance before the crew would accept him again.

Although hares have a number of pagan associations, they are occasionally found carved inside old village churches, together with the rare cat or deer, all symbolising magic and fertility in earlier eras. There are many Celtic and Roman illustrations of hares, appearing on wall paintings, as friezes and circling pottery jars, even as fine mosaics in some of the villas excavated in Britain.

St Patrick's Day

March is a month of change. It is possible to begin to see an awakening of Nature, and even when the weather is rainy or cool, there is a sense of expectancy because each day grows longer. By the end of the month the clocks have been put forward and the lighter evenings seem to promise better things to come. It is a time of coming together within families, especially around the old feasts of Mothering Sunday and for the Easter Holiday, if that should fall in March.

One of the green plants which is part of a celebration at this time is the Irish Shamrock, nowadays a kind of trefoil, but it might once have been the wood sorrel that was honoured. Saint Patrick was supposed to have chosen this three-leaved plant to represent the Christian Trinity, yet in the case of that other familiar triple-leaved plant, the clover, the occasional stem with four or five leaflets is considered lucky. St Patrick's Day is 17 March, and in New York and other places in America where many Irish people now live there are great parades when everyone wears green and has sprigs of 'Shamrock' about their person. Even the beer is dyed green for the occasion, although how it is possible to do this with dark Irish stout is another matter!

The Scottish Islanders and Highlanders also hold Patrick as important and celebrate his feast as the first day of the Northern Spring, finding salmon in the burns and newborn cattle and sheep in the byres. Patrick is supposed to have driven all the snakes out of Ireland; there aren't any there now. The other legend is that he turned the snakes to stone, which is the old explanation for those beautiful fossil ammonites found in many parts of the country, which look just like coiled snakes.

Mothering Sunday

The fourth Sunday in Lent is Mothering Sunday, traditionally a time when children returned to visit their mothers bearing small gifts of money, gloves or a posy of early Spring flowers. There was a reunion meal of some sort, which in the sparceness of the Lenten Fast was a great relief. There is a traditional cake baked at this time, called a 'Simnel' cake. Legend has it that this delicacy, usually covered with a crust of marzipan (called Marchpane in medieval times) was invented by a couple called Simon and Nell who couldn't agree how the cake should be cooked. One favoured baking, the other boiling, so both methods were used. Today, it is a rich fruit cake with a layer of marzipan in the middle as well as on top, where the almond paste is usually shaped into small balls or perhaps egg shapes. Again, these golden spheres appear at a time when it is traditional to recall the power of the Sun to shine on the world.

Mothering Sunday may fall about 25 March

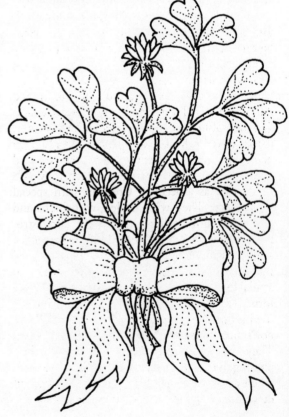

which is Lady Day, when the Virgin Mary received from the Archangel Gabriel (whose feast falls on 24 March) the Annunciation of the Birth of the Christ Child.

Spring Equinox and the Druids

The twenty-fifth of March was also an important date in medieval times, for it was taken as New Year's Day, and still is a Quarter Day when rents are due, although it ceased to be New Year's Day in 1752, when the calendars were changed. To people whose lives are ruled more directly by the movements of the Sun, 21 March, or thereabouts, is the Spring Equinox, when days and nights are of equal length, and it is when the Sun enters the Sign of Aries, the Ram, the first section of the Zodiacal Year, so in one sense it is indeed about the time of a new year.

Today, several of the small new Druid Orders, reformed in the eighteenth century, still hold public ceremonies to mark this date, in London and on some anciently sacred hill tops. Originally the Druids were a pre-Christian priesthood, found all over Europe, in the last thousand years before Christ. They saw the Sun in the sky as the symbol of a living power of Light, and most of their festivals were associated with the significant dates in the year, the Equinoxes in Spring and Autumn, when day and night are of equal length, and the Solstices at Midsummer and Midwinter. There were both male and female Druids, who had a long training, lasting many years, centred about Sacred Groves of trees, which they also reverenced as aspects of Creation with special significance. They were healers with herbs and practised 'faith healing', they were also astrologers. They kept verbal records of the descent of kings and ruling families and preserved the oral tradition of knowledge, learning by heart all available information, some constructed in verse form. They did know about forms of writing but used it only to pass messages to those who were not trained in the use of memory as they were. They held the scattered Celtic tribes together, blessing the newborn, attending funeral rites and, when occasion demanded, offering a white bull in sacrifice. Despite a bad press, begun by the Romans (who feared their magical powers, especially over the changeable Celtic weather) they have never burned people in woven baskets, although as upholders of the legal system of their age, they may have executed murderers or other felons. It would seem that the offering of a human life was only ever done in extreme circumstances, like that of the famous 'Pete Marsh', a preserved man from a Cheshire peat working, who was thought to have been a royal or Druidical sacrifice. It was made in desperate times when the Romans had slain thousands of Druids and other Celtic people all over Britain in 59 AD. Archaeological evidence produced from this rare find seems to indicate that the man was put to death about May Day, or Beltane, another important cross quarter festival, revered long before the Druid religion.

Although put down in many places by the Roman invasion, Druidism seems to have survived and in many ways blended with early Christianity in Britain, for married Druids often became early Bishops of the new church, and just as one Druid would pass on his parochial duties to his son, so Bishops continued the practice. It was only when the Church of Rome triumphed over the older, simpler Celtic Church, founded where St Joseph of Arimathea planted his ever-living thorn staff at Glastonbury, that priests had to cast off their wives and adopt many of the practices which continue to this day. It was at that time, in about the sixth century AD, that much of the magic and healing power fell away from the priesthood, to be returned to the simple country folk – the wise woman, the cunning men, the witches – who preserved it, in oral traditions, old feasts and local dances and tales, to modern times.

Easter Time

The date of Easter Sunday each year is still fixed with regard to the phases of the moon, which is why it shifts around quite a lot from year to year. Easter Sunday is the first Sunday after the full moon after the Spring Equinox, which falls around 21 March, so it always falls in a waning moon, traditionally a time when light turns inwards and enlightens the heart and spirit. Once the date of Easter itself has been established, then Lent and the preceding Forty Days are estimated; and the festivities which form the preparation for Lent, the Spring Cleaning, the Fast and the days of penance and purification can be worked out.

Traditionally most sowing of seed took place in March, weather permitting, and it was a time of great activity in the ploughlands. It was also a season where fertility of the soil and the livestock was prayed for, and this was made flesh in the hatching of chicks and ducklings about this time.

The Easter Bunny, probably really the magical hare mentioned before, is another very old symbol of fertility and multiplication, and so the chocolate ones on sale, especially from France, have far stronger pagan links with the rebirth of Nature than with the Christian festival.

Even the name Easter, used in Britain and other English speaking countries, is the name Eostra or Ostara, a Saxon Goddess of the Dawn of the Year. It has nothing whatever to do with the Passion and Death of Jesus. In other countries this feast is named more closely to 'passion', Pâques in French, and the Celtic and Gaelic names include Pascha, Pasg or Pasch, probably derived from the original *Pesach* in Hebrew, the Feast of Passover. Some local derivations include Peace and Pace, and there is a festival called 'Pace Egging' in many parts of Western and Northern England and Scotland.

The last Sunday before Easter is Palm Sunday in the Church calendar. It celebrates Jesus's arrival in Jerusalem, before the Jewish Feast of Passover. The Palm trees used in Britain are the fluffy, budded 'Pussy Willow' whose soft grey catkins are found on willows near water all over the country. In many churches, on this day, carefully woven 'palm crosses', made from fronds of Eastern palm trees, are given to the congregation. The gathering of early signs of spring, and the saving of the interlaced 'palm crosses', are both thought to bring luck and preserve the house from harm through the coming year.

Maundy Thursday

On Maunday Thursday, the Thursday before Easter Day, there is another extremely ancient custom, recorded as early as 600 AD, although its ritual has been simplified by now. The Sovereign gives out purses of Royal Maundy to poor people, the same number of deserving ladies and gentlemen as her years of age. In even-numbered years this takes place at Westminster Abbey and in odd-numbered years around the countryside. In earlier times the monarch not only distributed Maundy money, made up of symbolic coins, but washed, dried and kissed the feet of a number of poor people as an act of ritual humility. Sometimes a pair of slippers was given to each recipient as well as cash derived from the sale of the royal mantle, worn on the occasion. Queen Elizabeth I gave her poor subjects quite a mixed hamper; some money, an assortment of fish, including half a salmon, cloth to make a garment, a wooden dish of claret, an apron and the towel used in the washing ceremony, all contained in the original 'maund', a kind of wicker basket. Today the Queen gives each of the specially chosen recipients three leather purses; men getting two white and one red purse, and the ladies a green, a red and a white purse, containing specially minted Maundy Money. The colours of the purses are not those associated with money, such as gold or purple, but colours traditionally associated with the Goddess of Nature, or the Fairy Queen.

Good Friday

Good Friday comes next, the day beginning with a breakfast of Hot Crossed Buns, hot both in temperature and because they are spicy! Traditionally these were baked very early in the morning and vendors would walk the streets crying;

> Hot Crossed Buns, Hot Crossed Buns,
> One a penny, two a penny,
> Hot Crossed Buns
> If you have no daughters, give them
> to your sons,
> One a penny, two a penny,
> Hot Crossed Buns.

The round, spiced bun containing dried fruit and marked on top with a cross of white paste again predates the Christian feast, having been eaten at about the time of the Spring Equinox in honour of the Goddess of Spring. The Goddess controls the four seasons, hence the equal-armed cross. This same ancient symbol is frequently found on Celtic wayside stones and market crosses, and predates the Christian long-legged cross by many centuries. Hot Crossed Buns are attributed with healing properties and they will also last indefinitely if stored in a dry place. Some old churches and pubs have these relics preserved in their roofs, hanging in great clusters like musty brown grapes. Nowadays the shops have these seasonal buns for weeks both before Easter and long afterwards.

Good Friday, the day of Jesus's trial and crucifixion, is also the 'birthday' of the Holy Grail, that miraculous vessel which King Arthur's Knights sought as a panacea against the power of the Wasteland. One legend has it that it was originally the cup of the Last Supper which Joseph of Arimathea claimed after the Crucifixion, and which was eventually brought and concealed somewhere near Glastonbury. The Quest for the Holy Grail is an ongoing tradition recalled in song and story from Ireland to ancient Persia, and even as far east as China, where the Western Grail has become a rare pearl, again credited with the power of freeing the waters, restoring the land and healing the sick. Today we need that restorative essence even more than ever, for the Grail has never been found in a physical form, although various ancient contenders have been displayed at different times throughout history. The Grail of Jesus's Last Supper has an earlier counterpart yet – the Cauldron of Rebirth and Renewal, which was brought from the Otherworld, a parallel dimension of the Underworld of Earth.* Again this cauldron offers healing of the spirit and nourishment of the soul, both desperately needed in our materialistic world.

On Good Friday (originally God's Friday) churches are stripped of their bright symbols, bells are silent and all wait in tense expectancy for the crucifixion and death of Jesus, 'the Lamb of God who taketh away the sins of the world'. Lambs were sacrificed at this time, and still are in Greece, forming part of the special dishes eaten on Easter Day. In some churches Easter Grottoes are set out, decorated with primroses and catkins and bright green mosses, representing the rock tomb in which Jesus's body was laid, with its large stone covering the entrance. Although to some people this is a dark day, without the sacrifice there can be no resurrection, and without that there can be no redemption, within the concepts of the Christian faith.

Good Friday is also a time for special games, particularly Marbles; a championship game has been played in Tinsley Green, near Crawley in Sussex, for about four hundred years. Again, there may be a folk memory associating this season with sun symbols such as the small balls of marzipan on a Mothering Sunday cake, and the silver or gold balls used in Hurling or Football games.

Parsley was traditionally sown on Good Friday. Its seeds take a notoriously long time to germinate, and superstition had it that the Devil kept the seeds underground, or in Hell. Sowing the seeds on this holy day would foil the Devil and lead to an early sprouting. Today, pouring a kettle of boiling water over the seedbed immediately before the seeds are sown will have the same effect of preventing delay in the appearance of this tasty herb. You can sow dill, basil, chervil and thyme at the same time, if you wish to use these herbs later in the season. Most of them will start off better indoors, however. Outdoors, even a window box will provide enough space for a few plants of each variety.

* See *The Grail-Seekers Companion* by J. Matthews and M. Green.

Easter Saturday

The next day, Easter Saturday, also has its traditional games and dances in various parts of the country. One of the most colourful must be in Bacup where the Britannia Coconut Dancers perform with their flared red skirts, blackened hands and faces and 'coconuts' made out of weaving bobbins. During the dance, hands and knees strike up complex rhythms to the music of a band. These Coconut Dancers or 'Nutters' are only one of many forms of Morris Dancers which are to be found all over the country in ever-increasing numbers. Some sides are very ancient, tracing their tradition back to the middle ages; other new sides, including or exclusively of women dancers, are being formed all the time.

Easter Sunday

Easter Sunday is the climax of the Christian Festival, celebrated in churches throughout the land, with bell ringing, joyful singing and processions of candles all bringing the promise of resurrection and forgiveness of sins. After the days preceding the feast when the bright altar cloths had been removed and all flowers (except the sacrificial Easter Lilies) and pictures were absent, suddenly colour and light are restored, shining in the priest's vestments and the flower-filled niches. If the Sunday School children have made a grotto or miniature garden of the tomb of Christ, the stone is rolled away and the empty shroud is visible within, just as Mary Magdalene, that most faithful follower of Jesus, found it; she who questioned the angel who guarded the empty sepulchre, 'They have taken away the body of my Lord, and I know not where they have laid him.'

Early communities of monks used to enact this crucial part of the Christian story, using a high table altar with its covering turned back to represent the empty tomb, and from this simple enactment grew the celebration of Mystery Plays, and from them the whole of the Western theatre tradition sprang into being. Gradually the ritualised discovery of the open tomb and the message it sent forth began to be played out in the church porch, and later the street, with the actors climbing on to a cart for a stage. Soon the monks playing the holy characters gave way to Guildsmen who mimed parts of the Bible which concerned their trade or skill. The shipwrights might tell the story of Noah and the Flood, the Tanners act out the Fall of Lucifer, the Drapers the Creation, and the Bakers the Passion of Jesus. The great versions of the Mystery Cycles are still shown before considerable audiences, often out of doors, as were the original versions of the Chester, York and Coventry Mystery Plays.

Another, more pagan, series of traditional street theatricals are the various Mumming Plays, usually performed at Whitsun or Christmas. Their roots, however, lie in the religious theatre of Classical Greece, where performances were part of the pagan religion. Then they were used for healing as well as instruction, and taught the stories of the old gods, just as the early Mystery Plays enacted much of the Bible and New Testament.

In the Greek Orthodox Church the Easter Service takes place just after midnight when a new flame is lit, symbolising the Risen Christ. Each member of the congregation lights a taper and passes under the arch of a high altar in their own personal enactment of the rebirth into light.

Easter is a great time of revival and renewal of life. Around the country the traditional games and rituals reflect this celebration of the rebirth of Nature. There are games with balls, marbles, eggs, especially brightly coloured ones, symbolic hunts for hares and scrambling for hare pies. At Hallaton in Leicestershire they have 'bottle kicking'; fresh eggs are rolled down hills, 'shackled' or shaken in a flour sieve. Gorgeously decorated Easter bonnets, covered with flowers and ribbons, are traditionally worn for the first time to go to church on Easter Sunday.

The decorating of eggs has long been a common way of combining the artistic skill of children with this ancient symbol of fertility. Eggs are boiled with onion skins for a golden-brown colour, gorse flowers for yellow, cochineal for red and so on, or drawn on with a wax candle and then boiled in coloured water, with beetroot or any other natural dying material, to produce a pale pattern on a brighter eggshell. Goose eggs, being white, or duck eggs, sky blue, make delightful backgrounds for painting, when the blown shells are decorated with pictures and often adorned with sequins, gold braid and ribbon bows before being hung on a green branch to celebrate the return of Spring. The inside of the egg is used as one of the ingredients of Hot Crossed Buns.

Tradition has it that even the Sun dances for joy at the Resurrection, although the sky may be cloudy making it impossible to see; some worshippers would go to the top of a hill to witness this Mystery. Others watched in still water in a pool or basin drawn from an old spring, so that their sight was not harmed by gazing directly at the Sun's orb. This Rising Up theme was continued on Easter Monday and Tuesday in a curious custom called Easter Lifting or Heaving, when some young lads took a large chair to various houses and requested the ladies to take turns in being lifted up in it, to loud cheers, and for the price of a kiss. The next day the sporting ladies reversed the procedure. Sometimes small gifts of sweets or coins were exchanged for the kissing.

PISCES, THE FISH

Most of March is under the constellation of Pisces, the Fish. This, like Libra and Gemini, is a double sign; it is represented in most old depictions as fish swimming in opposite directions to each other. This is reflected in the character of those born between roughly 20 February and 21 March. Pisceans are ruled by the two planets Jupiter and Neptune, adding to the dual nature of the sign. Pisces is also associated with Water, showing that feelings and emotions play an important part in their lives. As characteristics are developed as the circle of the zodiac passes, those in the later signs, Capricorn, Aquarius and Pisces tend to be more complicated people, or folk with fingers in many pies. Because Pisces is ruled by the planet, Jupiter, which looks after the material things in life, job, possessions, position in the world, Pisces people can be extremely successful in their field of work. However, because it is also a water sign, they tend towards those kinds of professions or careers where service is of greater importance than money.

In this, as in other aspects of this sometimes contradictory sign (the Fishes are always shown swimming in opposite directions), Pisceans need to be able to choose. Unlike the equally twinned Libra sign, the Fish folk can usually make up their minds quickly, but the basis upon which they make decisions tends to be intuitive rather than pure reason.

Some Pisceans have rather pale complexions, or fair hair, their movements may seem clumsy, as if they are not really moving in their own element, yet they can be graceful dancers and enjoy movement. The things they most like are enduring ones for they have great patience and a quiet passivity, preferring to let things come to them, rather than actively seeking them out. This applies in the field of friendship, too, for though they are generous and humorous they often prefer their own company.

Again, because Neptune, the planet of visions, dreams, intuition and hallucination may be a strong influence in their lives, if it is well aspected to other planets, these people can be very dreamy and detached, drifting through life in an other-worldly way. They can be moody, yet their dreams can be creative, when they can find the energy to make them come true. They are poetic, philosophical, romantic and influenced by others around them, for good or ill. They can be very perceptive concerning the feelings of others and they may have active psychic and even visionary and mediumistic tendencies which need to be controlled by commonsense.

They are kind, gentle people, caring for children and animals, yet can be tough and determined if their position is threatened. They again excel in the field of music, counting Handel, Chopin and Rossini among their number. Albert Einstein, Michaelangelo, Ibsen and Longfellow were also born at this time of year.

For occupations, Pisceans are keen on anything to do with water, although on the whole they are not very keen on competitive sports, preferring the quiet meditation of fishing beside a gentle stream to winning prizes for water skiing! They also like travel, and working with wines or animals. They make good priests, combining sensitivity with sympathy, and excellent nurses; in fact most caring professions will suit anyone with Pisces dominant in their chart.

The jewels associated with Pisces include sapphires and emeralds with their watery colours; but rich, purple amethysts, the gems of the planet Jupiter, and coral for Neptune, would always make acceptable gifts.

Simnel Cake

This cake is no longer baked and boiled as it used to be, but it is still made in two layers, stuck together with a circle of marzipan, and decorated with marzipan spheres or egg-shapes.

Cake

6 oz/175g/1½ cups self-raising flour
pinch of salt
½ tsp each grated nutmeg, ground ginger, mixed spice and cinnamon
6 oz/175g/¾ cup butter
6 oz/175g/1 firmly-packed cup brown sugar
3 eggs
8 oz/250g/1½ cups mixed, dried fruit
4 oz/125g/⅓ cup apricot jam

Marzipan

1 lb/500g/4 cups ground almonds
1 lb/500g/3½ cups icing or confectioner's sugar
½ tsp each vanilla and almond essence
1 tbsp lemon juice
2 egg yolks
1 egg white, beaten

Sift together the flour, salt and spices. Cream the butter and sugar until fluffy. Beat in the eggs and then fold in the flour mixture and the dried fruit. Grease two 8-inch/20-centimetre cake tins and divide the mixture between them. Bake in a preheated 325°F/170°C/ Mark 3 oven for about 45 minutes. Cool the cakes completely and then spread their sides and tops with the apricot jam.

To make the marzipan, mix together the ground almonds and icing sugar, gradually adding the vanilla and almond essences, the lemon juice and the egg yolks, beating until a stiff paste is formed. Divide the marzipan into three equal parts and lightly roll out two of these on an icing-sugar dusted surface. You need two circles that will just cover the cakes. Make a stack of cake, marzipan, cake and finally marzipan. The last portion of marzipan may be tinted with edible food colouring, if you wish; then form it into egg or sphere shapes. Decorate the top of the cake with these shapes. Coat the top and decorations with the beaten egg white, place the cake on a baking tray, and put into a preheated 450°F/230°C/ Mark 8 oven for about 5 minutes to glaze the top.

Cawl

This is a traditional dish to serve on St David's Day, 1 March.

1 lb/500g/2½ cups diced best end of neck of lamb
½ lb /250g/1 cup diced bacon
Oil
Salt and pepper
1 lb/500g/2½ cups diced potatoes
½ lb/250g/1 cup sliced leeks
½ lb/250g/1½ cups chopped onions
½ lb/250g/1 cup diced carrots, swede or turnip

Heat a little oil in a frying pan and brown the diced lamb in it. Place the lamb and bacon plus seasoning in a large stewpan and cover with water. Simmer for one hour. Add the vegetables and simmer for another hour. Serve the cawl hot with fresh bread.

Oranges and Lemons for St Clements

Actually this is grapefruit and orange, but it can be decorated with thin circles of lemon and orange to make it more appropriate. Cut a large sweet grapefruit in half and spread a good spoonful of thick-cut homemade marmalade, or Oxford marmalade, on each half. Place the fruit under a hot grill for a few moments until the marmalade is bubbling. Place each half in a serving dish and decorate with fresh orange and lemon slices.

HOW TO MAKE A SPRING KITE

Kites have always been flown in the Spring, on clear, windy days. In some parts of the world competitions and kite festivals are held, when the skies are full of bright, flying shapes.

This design is for a simple diamond-shaped traditional kite which can be made from scrap material or recycled plastic shopping bags. You will need two light but stiff sticks or green garden canes, one about a quarter longer than the other, some string, sticky tape and a couple of plastic shopping bags or a piece of thin material. First cross the two sticks with the shorter one above the middle of the longer one, and tie or tape firmly. Take a length of string and tape it or tie it carefully to the four ends of the sticks to make a taut kite-shape. Lay the tied sticks on to the flattened material or opened out plastic bag, and cut a piece about an inch (2 to 3 centimetres) larger than the kite frame. Clip the material to the frame at the four points, fold the plastic over the string shape and carefully stick with tape or sew it over the string.

Attach a 'bridle' of string to the longer stick above and below the cross piece, ideally through the covering material so that the wind hits the plain side of the kite when it is flown. Next, make a tail out of bows of strips of plastic knotted onto a string and tie this at the bottom corner of the kite, through the covering material. Tie the flying line of string to the 'bridle' and on a windy day, in a place well clear of any trees or overhead wires or obstructions, get a friend to help you launch your new toy. You may need to adjust the length of the tail, or the angle of the 'bridle', to make it fly well.

Miniature kites may be made of drinking straws with paper, cloth or plastic covers as decorations for a party, and these can be flown by whirling them round on their strings. All kites may be decorated with faces, birds or anything you fancy, sewn or stuck onto the face of the kite.

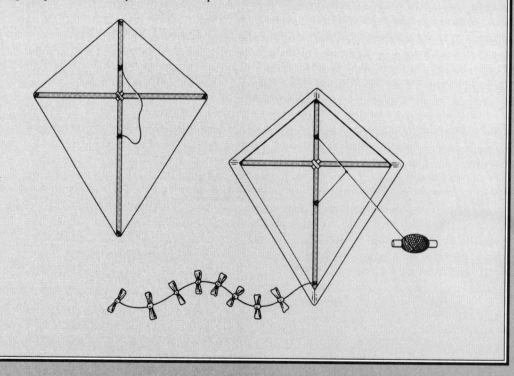

36

APRIL

This April, with his stormy showers,
Doth make the Earth yield pleasant flowers ...

Neve's '*Almanack*', 1633

Showery, flowery April is a month of contrasts. The green gauzy veil of Mother Nature is floating over all the fields and woodlands, filling the whole countryside with verdant light. It is a time of bright, windy blue skies and the sudden dark clouds and heavy showers which differentiate this month from all others. It is a playful month, yet T.S. Eliot in his powerful work 'The Wasteland' saw it as a cruel month, a time of promises unfulfilled and the warmth of Spring denied or delayed until the approach of May.

The new greenery is studded everywhere with glints of gold, lesser celandines under the hedges, woods full of the pale primrose paths to dalliance; old meadows, or more often, these days, motorway verges, patterned with shy cowslips. Coppiced woodlands shimmer with hazel catkins and flutter with white wild wood anenomes, waterways in unpolluted places reflect the shiny golden flowers of marsh marigolds. Daisies star every lawn and wallflowers scent the garden borders, already burgeoning with the buds of flowers to come.

All Fools' Day

The first of April some do say,
Was set apart as All Fools' Day,
But why the people call it so,
Nor I nor they themselves do know!

This much an eighteenth century rhymer tells us. Perhaps the origins of this lighthearted day stem from the joy of Easter, often about this time, or at least from the relief that warmer days and new growth are overhauling the bleakness of winter, which used to seem to the old agricultural society to drag on endlessly. Nearly all pagan religions have a God associated with jokes, disguises, mischief or making fun of people, and it is his festival which is still celebrated on this morning, for all jokes are stale by twelve noon.

In the past, apprentices were sent to shops to buy 'A pound of glass nails and a rubber hammer to knock them in with.' Today some of these practical but harmless japes have been updated, and a young worker might be sent to a factory's store to collect ten kilos of expanded polystyrene, which if it were in stock would be about the size of a room! Today it is the newspapers and television which have taken up the challenge to fool as many people as possible, showing the harvesting of spaghetti from the vines, or the rare animal in the zoo, the 'Lirpa Loof'. In the North, Hunting the Gowk, or cuckoo, was a tradition for this day. The feckless messenger would be sent from one fruitless destination to another, enquiring after the Gowk's whereabouts, until he twigged it was a trick and he himself the subject of the search! Nowadays, the message is doubtless relayed by fax! Although some tricks were cruel, the best were always those most carefully thought out and which tricked the most people. But at lunchtime the game had to stop and anyone trying to catch you out after then would be declared an April Noddy himself.

Carnival

As Easter often falls in April, some of the associated festivals and traditions are transferred to the beginning of this month. One of the most famous, celebrated in many parts of the world, is 'Carnival', the Latin words for 'Farewell to meat!', originally the beginning of the Lenten Fast. From Rio de Janeiro in Brazil to New Orleans in America and Venice in Italy this is a great occasion. It is a time for music and dancing, and especially for donning the most elaborate costumes and masks and parading, partying and showing yourself off. The domino or half-mask used to be very popular, but it was held on a stick, thus denying the wearer the use of one hand most of the evening. Later full face masks were worn, often covering the face down to the mouth, which had to be free for drinking, eating and kissing! Today these carnival masks have become a minor industry and shops all over the place are selling original, antique masks, usually favouring Sun or Moon faces, white-faced clowns or gorgeously decorated harlequins, as well as modern versions.

Masks have always played an important part in ritual, folk customs and early drama, which in ancient Greece formed an essential aspect of religious practice. Each actor, playing his part in the stories of Gods or heroes, wore his mask, the 'Persona'. This is now a familiar term used in psychology to indicate the face we wear in public. The traditional twin masks of comedy and tragedy deck the prosceniums of many a theatre in Europe, reflecting this desire by the actors, and the world at large, to display a face other than that of their true personalities.

Dressing up, too, forms an on-going part of many festivities, whether it is the adoption of a particular costume (like that of the Morris Dancers, of mainly white, with flowers, bells and ribbons in varying colours for each 'Side'), or some sort of disguise. Guisers (sometimes pronounced 'geezers') often wore ragged garments, or clothes covered with strips of paper or cloth.

They might wear the traditional jester's motley, red and yellow parti-coloured costumes, with a threefold hat with bells on the points, or ordinary clothing, worn inside out or back to front. This old custom was used as a way to deflect the gaze of someone who might wish you harm, or the evil eye. Particularly in Scotland the reversing of coats or jackets was done to ward off bad luck, and in many places the face would be blacked with soot. Some of the special festival dance troups would black up, partly for luck and partly as a disguise, and it may have been this tradition which gave Morris or Moorish dances their name, from the dark faced 'Black-a-moors' who were the earliest visitors to Britain long ago. Children always seem to love dressing up, in grown-ups' clothes, or for school plays, or charades, so this idea is deeply embedded in our inherited memory.

Horses

One event which attracts a lot of public attention at the beginning of April is the famous horserace the Grand National, held at Aintree Racecourse near Liverpool. Unlike any other worldwide, this testing race pits the courage and strength of jumping horses with the fitness and determination of their jockeys, over four and a half miles and thirty fences, on the first Saturday in April. It also has a long history: having been run in a different form in about 1830, it gained the name 'Grand Liverpool Steeplechase' at Aintree in 1839. It was on this occasion that Captain Becher fell into the stream which crosses the course, and it is still known as Becher's Brook. Other fences include Valentine's Brook, The Chair Fence, which is the narrowest on the course, and the Canal Turn. In recent years some of the danger has been reduced at these formidable obstacles, hopefully making it a safer race for horses and jockeys alike, which is especially important. A number of women riders have completed the Course as well.

Although the Grand National is one of the horse races which has made this industry internationally known, it is very different in spirit to the elegant summer 'flat' races at Ascot, Epsom and Newmarket. The Grand National is a 'people's' race, with older, tougher horses probably well known from the racing pages of the papers from the preceding winter, when they have to qualify over a similar distance or course. Many people who usually have nothing to do with racing or betting join in an office sweepstake, or place a bet on a horse because they like its name, or the colours its jockey will be wearing. Thousands flock to the course, and thrill to the spectacle of thirty horses flying over the huge fences with their uncommon covering of loose spruce and evergreen branches. That feeling of excitement – there whether the race is watched on television or seen in person – seems to be another of our inherited urges.

Horses have been a part of human activities for a very long time, and though now we usually see them only as a form of entertainment, as hacks to ride at the local Equestrian Centre, as show jumpers, race horses or the huge Shires or Percherons hauling drays for the brewery, in Britain and Ireland we have always had a special feeling for them. We do not, as a nation, eat horse flesh, although it is a delicacy in much of Europe, and it is on those tables that some of our own horses and ponies may end up! Our Celtic ancestors were great horsemen, and though the animals they rode before the Romans came were only ponies by modern standards, they were tough working beasts, and fast enough to race, whether ridden or as chariot ponies. At every Celtic king's funeral, equestrian events formed part of the Funeral Games, with horse races and chariot driving contests; and spear throwing and archery games played whilst mounted on a galloping steed.

The horse has a deeply embedded place in our folklore too, turning up as the vast chalk-cut figure near Uffington in Wiltshire, where the shape of a galloping horse can be seen from miles away. There was an ancient horse goddess, too, called Epona by the Romans, bestowing blessings of peace and fertility on her worshippers. Horse figurines have turned up in many ancient archaeological digs, and as decoration on armour and pottery; as well as quantities of horse harness itself. This is often beautifully decorated with enamel inlay and semi-precious stones, showing that the owners were proud of their chariot teams or riding horses.

In many of the dances, processions and ongoing seasonal customs a horse figure is found, standing in for death-and-rebirth, for growth and for luck and fertility, which in earlier times went hand-in-hand. Many Morris sides have a 'hobby horse', these days not always just a horse but, like the Westminster Men, a glorious Unicorn, or the Exeter's Morris stag. At Padstow it is the round, black 'Obby 'Oss who is the leader of the dance, and at Minehead, the horse-cum-boat celebrates the return of spring. Some of the earliest medieval pictures of fools show them with the Hobby Horse (we know it as a child's toy now); a horse head on a stick, ridden as if it were a real steed.

The horse is also associated with the power of the land, and in ancient coronation ceremonies it was by a symbolic, sacred marriage to a white mare that the Kings of our land held their power. It may be for this reason that many public houses throughout our land are named The White Horse, The Black Horse, The Nag's Head and so on. Perhaps these were originally gathering places when horses were so much more important to people's lives and work, forming the centre of territories. Certainly many huge hill figures, both undeniably ancient and relatively modern, have chosen to depict a white horse, although on different soils there have been red horses too.

Children probably still dream of learning to ride, of having a pony in a shed at the bottom of the garden, or of being able to spend holidays riding over moors and countryside where wild ponies live freely and proudly in scattered herds among the heather. A horse offers a silent companionship, a mutual support and gentle comfort to those who care for them, as well as freedom to go cross country, to gallop along deserted beaches or on the old green roads, built when the first magical white horse shapes were cut from the turf. Horses haunt our dreams too, as symbols of power, venturing into the unknown and, depending on the psychologists' interpretations, sex or success.

Nature's Scene

April is perhaps the most beautiful of spring's months, for the flowers are spreading their petals and the earliest trees are veiled in a green gossamer gown. The sharp showers scent the air with fresh-turned earth and the perfume of early blossom, where the sun catches it. It is a time when many birds put in a summer appearance, and the echoing calls of the cuckoo, that mysterious wanderer with unpleasant, murderous tendencies, may be heard announcing the arrival of summer in every valley and wood. To our ancestors April must have brought relief from the cold and fear of winter starvation, for the grass is usually greening by now and life everywhere is taking up its cycle of rebirth.

The earliest greenery that can be eaten can now be found. Young nettles, found on wasteland, can be eaten as a vegetable or made into nettle beer. Nettles are rich in iron and other vitamins, as are the unfurling buds of hawthorn leaves, known in some places as 'bread and cheese', and another welcome addition to a deficient diet.

The Enigma of Shakespeare

As the weather starts to improve and work out of doors begins to occupy more time and effort, as the evenings lengthen, 'and showers betumble the chestnut spikes, and nestlings fly ..' it is a time of poetic inspiration and writing of flowery verses. One famous name whose birthday is celebrated in April is William Shakespeare, whose day coincides with that of the patron saint of England, St George, on 23 April. Shakespeare is still an enigmatic character and though his works are known and enjoyed worldwide, his very existence is still a matter of great debate. In Stratford-upon-Avon visitors can see his school desk, his home and that of his wife, they can watch his plays, read his verses, and yet the person, depicted on so many souvenirs, may evade them altogether. What adds to the mystery of this prolific writer is that none of his works survive in his handwriting, but appear in print in the famous First Folio, issued in 1623, long after the year of his death. His thirty-seven well-known plays, the comedies, the tragedies and the historic plays, must have all had some common author, yet nowhere are there working scripts, no rough copies scribbled on the backs of old play bills.

Shakespeare is an industry. His home town has become a shrine and place of pilgrimage for people from all over the world. And yet the more closely you look at William Shakespeare the playwright, poet and travelling player, the more invisible he becomes. Certainly great literary minds of our own era have offered alternative writers (Roger Bacon, for example, or the Earl of Oxford) as the real writers of all these plays. Computers have analysed the style, the language and the format of all the known works, and technical equipment has x-rayed the memorial plaque behind which it was presumed his bones or his manuscripts rested, all to no avail. Some scholars have devoted their entire lives to un-covering who the real William Shakespeare might have been, and put forth some strange options, including the notion that the plays were a part-time hobby of Queen Elizabeth I, or that they were really the works of other Acting Companies of the latter half of the sixteenth century.

Whatever else he, or perhaps she, might have been, Shakespeare was a magician, immersed in those hidden aspects of people's lives, their dreams and visions, their aims and attitudes. Although now it is literary experts and scholars who are keenest on his works, in the sixteenth century the plays were performed as entertain-ment for the common folk, and the in-jokes and situations portrayed must have been familiar to them. Shakespeare was well-versed in the secret side of life too, for his witches in Macbeth have become almost archetypal of witches every-where, stirring their pot on the blasted heath, making potions from herbs and mushrooms and all kinds of evil-sounding things (many of which are in fact common names for plants and weeds!) He has ghosts in several plays – Macbeth and Hamlet for example – and he has fairies and spirits in others – Midsummer Night's Dream and the Tempest. Several of his works show some deeper knowledge of astrology and alchemy; occasionally he dresses his characters in the colours and guises of the planets and heavenly bodies.

Disguise and transformation scenes, ladies dressing as men, characters becoming animals, as Bottom does in Midsummer Night's Dream – with these ruses Shakespeare appeals to the inner senses of the audience in just the same way that makers of science fiction and fantasy films do today. It is this timeless and unchanging theme of myth that Shakespeare and other writers have continued to exploit in theatre, literature and poetic tale through all the ages. It still entertains us because at some inner level of our own beings we sense an enduring truth within the story. Love conquering all, evil being ousted, equity and law triumphing over darkness and dispute. The themes remain. 'In Spring the young man's fancy turns to love.' 'If music be the food of love, play on ..' 'All the world's a stage and men and women merely players ...'

On Shakespeare's birthday there is a procession through Stratford on Avon to the church where a wreath of flowers is laid. The twenty-third of April is the date of his death, as well as his birth, according, if not to fact, to scholarly decision. From the registering of his Baptism on 26 April, 1564, to his death in 1616, his exact life story has remained a mystery, yet the vast richness of literature attributed to his quill is the cause for celebrating festivals all over the world. From school children to dedicated theatre companies, people need to remember William Shakespeare, whoever he may have been.

Saint George and the Dragon

Saint George, the patron saint of England, is another mysterious character, as most saints are. He was reputed to have rescued the daughter of the king of Silene, sometime at the end of the third century AD. The maiden was a sacrificial victim offered to a dragon which was devouring the people. St George arrived on his white horse, in some versions beheaded the dragon with his sword, in others pierced it through with a spear, and thus saved the young lady. John Aubrey, writing in the 1680s, was doubtful about the truth of the tale:

To save a Mayd, St George the Dragon slew,
A pretty tale, if all is told be true,
Most say There are no Dragons; and tis sayd
There was no George; Pray God there was a Mayd!

St George slaying the dragon is the symbol attached to the collar worn by the Order of the Garter, a most noble and exclusive company, of which there are normally only twenty-six knights, including the sovereign. This, like so many parts of our pageantry history, has roots in folklore, for the idea was conceived when a lady, at a dance, lost her garter. The King, Edward III, picked it up and is reputed to have said 'Honi soit qui mal y pense', which is now the motto of the Order.

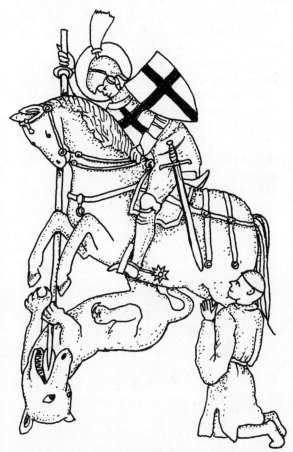

establishments use a staff with two intertwined snakes, borrowed from the god of communication, Hermes, as their logo.

There are many old tales of heroes tackling dragons and giants, in the Arthurian legends, for example; or lake monsters, in Celtic myth, or even the Lambton Worm. Great Orm's Head is named after a serpentine dragon, and of course this mysterious beast, complete with wings (for the European dragons, unlike their ancient Chinese counterparts, could fly) still appears on the flag of the Welsh nation. King Arthur's father was Uther Pendragon, for this was used as a title of a warrior lord. Dragons in various forms still haunt us, for the quest for the Loch Ness Monster has not been concluded, and perhaps a newer sign of dragon tracks from the sky might be the many occurrences in recent years of circles and other strange patterns in cornfields, particularly in Southern England. There is a hill close to the White Horse of Uffington called Dragon Hill, on which nothing will grow. This is where, legend has it, St George slew his dragon.

Beating the Bounds

At this time of renewal, when nightingales' and cuckoos' songs fill the valleys, and animals and birds have paired off and are seeing about rearing their young, it was traditional at Rogationtide to renew the people's memories of parish and other boundaries. This is called 'Beating the Bounds' in some places, when the parish priest and choir took long hazelwood poles and walked the boundaries of their parish, beating the boundary markers, stones, fences or streams and, occasionally, thrashing these marks into the heads of the congregation, both children and adults. In Cambridgeshire it was customary to bump a young chorister head down on the boundary stone, perhaps recalling an ancient offering when a child was left in a nearby hollow as a sacrifice to the powers which maintain safe boundaries. Sometimes coins or sweets are used as an inducement to the people to recall the limits of their territory, and suitable hymns are sung and relevant passages from the Bible recall the importance of knowing where one's limits are set.

Dragons are deeply embedded in folk memory. They are carved on many ancient churches, usually being overcome by either St George, the Dragon Slayer, or St Michael the balancer of light and darkness, who stands above, but does not necessarily kill, his dragon-assailant. Recent research has indicated that the dragon represented the life force of the Earth, a wild and free magical spirit which was depicted in various ways at many seasonal gatherings. In some medieval traditions the dragon was equated with Satan, the fallen angel, and Lord of the World, but there seems to be an older tradition where the healing power of worms, serpents and dragons was sought, both on an individual level, for curing sickness, and on a greater scale, to heal droughts or plagues in the land. A single snake is seen coiled round the staff of the Greek healing god, Asclepius, whose statues are found in several ancient sites in Britain, including at the healing hot spring in Bath. Even now many medical

The End of April

At the end of April, with the warmth of summer approaching, and the spreading colours of wild flowers touching the verdant meadows with a brush of many colours, it is a time of hope and beauty. Poets of all kinds wrote of its sweetness, sometimes tinged with bitterness. The Swan of Avon wrote of the sad songs of nightingales, which in sixteenth century England were not considered romantic, as the one which sang in Berkeley Square later on was, but as symbolising loneliness and melancholy. Plants that flower this month include the sunlight-reflecting yellow primroses and marsh marigolds, called in some places 'water bubbles' from their aquatic environment. Among the woodland primroses are to be found the white wood anemones, touched with purple at their throats, and the star-like flowers of spring squill. The hazel catkins shake their golden pollen and those who study the still bare twigs of this useful tree will see the tiny scarlet stars of the female flowers. The mysterious chequered bells of the fritillary, seen now more often in its cultivated forms in gardens, shakes its purple and white bowed heads towards the end of April.

The last days of April formed an important watershed in the natural year of the pre-Christian Celts, for like Hallowe'en, at the beginning of winter, the April/May tide, as we know it now from our modern calendars, marked the transition from winter to summer. It was a time of great release, when the penned cattle, sheep and pigs could be taken out into the open pastures and woodland, where enough new grass and other greenery was there to support them. It was a time when work and living was carried out mainly in the open air after the smokey winter life within the walls of houses and byres.

The church was concerned about this imminent freedom and warned its followers of the great evils abroad on St Walpurgis Night, because the veil between the real world and the Otherworld was particularly thin at this season. There are many customs carried out at the end of the month to do with ghosts, like that of keeping watch on St Mark's eve, on 24 April, from the church porch, if you dare, to see the shades of those who are laid to rest in the hallowed loam in the coming twelvemonth. If any spirits enter the church yard but then leave again, it shows that though these folk may be ill during the year, they will survive. In the two hours around midnight those who were to pass on were expected to make their presence felt, and if you were to be a victim yourself you might encounter your own ghost! To bring better luck many people went out on the next day, which was St Mark's feast, and gathered the scented gold of cowslips (originally cow slops – thought to grow where cows had left their mark in the pastures) to make wine.

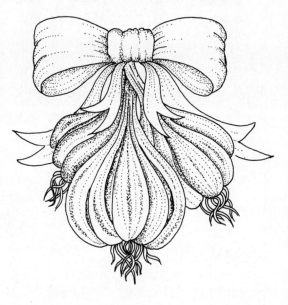

To ensure that no harm entered your home in the month when 'The cowslips about and the bullrushes out!' you should hang garlic or onions about the cradle or beds of your children. Or you should seek out a rowan tree you had never seen before, take two twigs and bind them into an equal-armed cross with red wool or thread, and hang this over the main door of your dwelling. You could take extra precautions by going to bed with a piece of stale breadcrust dipped in salt under your pillow or a bare, steel knife blade pointing north near you, or an open Bible to ward off any harmful influences. With any luck these precautions would keep you safe to be up early to celebrate the rites of May Day, when you should bathe your face in the dew.

ARIES, THE RAM

April is mostly ruled by the zodiac sign Aries, the Ram, and forms the first part of the star-led year. Aries is a fire sign, showing the energy of the growing strength of the sun, and the determination to overcome the darkness of winter. It is a lusty time, and those born under this sign tend to be go-ahead people, innovative and sometimes very keen to see their ideas or principles upheld, come what may. It is ruled by the planet Mars and associated with the colour red and the metal iron. This may show that Aries people seek association with the armed forces, with industry and with mechanical equipment. They may not have the subtle approach of those whose natal signs are ruled by air or water, but their go-ahead manner can often get them into positions of leadership or control.

Aries people can be very forthright in their dealings with others because if Mars, the planet of energy, is well aspected in their charts, they will have a great deal of self-confidence and self-assurance. Both men and women have a great sense of adventure, liking to explore new places and make an impact on new company. Of course, in extremes they can be rash or fanatical over something which interests them, or they may be ruthless in the way they cope with situations. In other circumstances this aspect of their natures can come over as criticism, sharp-tongued and sarcastic, or defiance and lack of co-operation, especially when they are young, and feel they are being thwarted by their elders and betters.

Those born in Aries are often very handsome or beautiful, with dark hair, a healthy outdoor look to them, for most of these people enjoy out of door activities, where they can show off their natural strengths and athletic prowess. They do like to show off. Many of them have red glints in their hair which is very striking in sunlight, and demonstrates their inner fire and energy. Because they enjoy all kinds of challenges some Aries people have scars on their faces which are the result of over ambitious acts or dangerous hobbies.

The sign of the Ram rules the head, and it is thought that those whose horoscope shows them to be Ariens may suffer headaches, or perhaps short-sightedness. They may also be head-strong and get themselves worked up by worrying about their position in their job or family, leading to stress and anxiety. If they take a few tips from the sheep in the field and learn to sit down quietly and chew things over, or ruminate, they will gain control over such troublesome attitudes. Aries folk can be good and reliable friends, so long as they get their own way fairly often, and they do appreciate being recognised for their new or valuable suggestions. As marriage partners, however, they need understanding and consideration, and either an equally determined partner who will fight his or her own corner, or someone who is happy to follow their lead.

The gem stones associated with Aries are rubies, diamonds and bloodstones, and Ariens often like bright colours, especially most forms of red, including muted pinks and vivid orange. Many of them look good in white, with other colours, such as bright green, to relieve the starkness. They are one of the few signs that even brilliant yellow may suit, and they can wear startling colour combinations and not be afraid of being looked at; in fact they very much enjoy showing off.

APRIL RECIPES

Duck with Cider

1 duck approximately 5 lb/2.5kg
2 apples, cored and sliced
12fl oz/35 cl/1½ cups cider
salt and pepper

Season the duck with salt and pepper. Fill the cavity with the apple slices, and secure with a skewer. Put the duck on a rack in a roasting pan and pour the cider over it. Put in a preheated 325°F/170°C/Mark 3 oven and roast for 2½ hours or until done. Baste the duck with the liquid every 15 minutes. When the bird is cooked, transfer it to a carving board and keep hot until you serve it.

April Apricot Fool

Pour the juice off a tin of apricot halves. Put the fruit into a blender with one teaspoonful of clear honey, and purée. Stiffly whip ½ pint/30cl/1⅓ cups of double cream and carefully fold in the puréed fruit until completely mixed. Pour into four stemmed glasses and decorate as foolishly as you can, with cocktail umbrellas, faces drawn in food colouring or with 'hundreds and thousands'.

Dry Dandelion Wine

4 pints/2.5 litres/5 cups dandelion flowers
   (as little green as possible)
One 1 inch/2.5 centimetre piece root
   ginger, bruised
4 pints/2.5 litres/5 US pints water
2 oranges
2 lemons
3½ lbs/1.75kg/7 cups white sugar
1½ tsp wine yeast, activated in a little warm
   water

Put the yellow heads in a large bowl with the ginger. Bring the water to the boil, pour it over the dandelions and stir. Cover and leave for two to three days, stirring occasionally.

Thinly peel the rinds of the oranges and lemons, and strain and reserve the juice. Strain the dandelion liquid into a large pan, add the orange and lemon rinds, and bring to the boil. Simmer for 10 minutes, then strain it on to the sugar and stir. When cool, pour it into a warm fermentation jar, and add the orange and lemon juice and the activated yeast. Insert the airlock and allow to ferment to a finish in a warm place. Stand in a cool place for about a week to settle out before bottling.

Nettle Quiche

Nettles are said to taste rather like spinach when cooked, and they are very nutritious.

8″ pastry shell, baked blind
8 oz/250g young nettle shoots
1 onion
1 oz/30g butter
2 eggs
½ pint/30cl milk
2 oz/65g grated cheese
salt, pepper, mixed herbs to taste

Choose only young nettle shoots, taking the top four leaves. Wash and cook in salted water for ten minutes, then drain. They will now have lost their sting. Cook for a few minutes to evaporate any liquid, then transfer to the pastry case. Beat together the eggs, milk, salt and pepper and pour over the nettles. Sprinkle with cheese and mixed herbs to taste and bake for 25 to 30 minutes at 200°C/400°F/Gas Mark 6.

MAY

A fair maid who, the first of May
Goes to the fields at break of day
And washes in dew 'neath the hawthorn tree
Will ever after handsome be.

Country saying

The month of May, when the grass is covering the meadows like emerald velvet, and buds on trees and plants swell almost as you watch them, really begins to feel like summer. May was always a time of great relief in the agricultural communities because it was possible to feel the warmth in the air which helped the crops to make headway after a very long time of darkness and dearth. Those who cared for their skin, maids and married ladies alike, would be out before sunrise, seeking a dewy patch of grass, or dew drops from the petals of early flowers, to bathe their faces and eyes and bring them to a petal-like beauty of smoothness and rosy health. Perhaps it helped.

Others would be out in the woods, seeking the first blossoms of scented hawthorn, the May tree, for it was really the blooming of this hedge plant which marked the transition from winter to summer, rather than the calendar date. 'Cast not a clowt 'til May be out', wise advice on the matter of putting aside the winter woollies, referred surely to the flowers rather than the month. May Day has been a festival in many European communities for thousands of years, and regular festivities of all kinds were to be seen across the countryside. Some were processions, others dances, and in villages and towns the young May Queen was elected and ceremonially crowned, as

the merry month progressed. Merry, as in Merry or even Merrie England relates to Fairy, and it was a time when the magic of the Fairy Queen, the White Lady, was to be seen across the land.

Rudyard Kipling caught something of the spirit of the old pagan rite of 'A Maying' when he wrote:

O do not tell the priest our plight,
For he would call it sin,
For we've been out in the woods all night,
A 'conjuring summer in.
I bring good news by word of mouth,
Good news for cattle and corn,
For now is the sun come out of the South,
With Oak, and Ash, and Thorn.

Here are two anciently observed principles, one is the signs of spring heralded by the greening or flowering of oak and ash and thorn trees, and the other is 'the sun coming out of the South'.

The Line of Sunrise

Recent research has begun to unravel a great mystery which crosses the southern part of Britain from Cornwall to East Anglia. It is a line of ancient churches dedicated to many of the Christian saints whose roles took over aspects of the power previously attributed to the Sun God. There are many churches, chapels and ruins whose dedication is to St Michael, always linked with fire and with overcoming the power of the serpent; St George, whose name may have been derived from 'Og', the Scottish Gaelic Sun God, and St Mary, whose many attributes of Ever Virgin, Star of the Sea and Mother of God give her an important part in any religion where a female principle is worshipped. Running from St Michael's Mount off Cornwall, via Glastonbury and the vast circle of standing stones and man-made mounds at Avebury, the line continues diagonally through over sixty churches, including Ogbourne St George, to go to sea over Hopton in Suffolk. What links all these holy places together is the visible line of sunrise at the beginning of the month of May. If a beacon fire were lit upon each high point the sun would be seen to rise behind it viewed from the next place along a line.

Beltane

Here in Britain, there is an ancient connection of sacred sites, old churches and the pre-Christian mounds they occupy, which seems to acknowledge an older power of light, visible around May Day, and again about the start of August, Lammastide, which is traditionally the beginning of harvest. The old name for the feast at the beginning of May was Beltane, variously spelt, but consisting of two components, Bel and Tan. Bel is known to be an ancient Sun God name, closely associated with the older title, *Baal*, meaning Lord in Phoenician. *Tan* is Celtic for Fire, so here there is a double principle of God, or good, if you take the French concept, and Fire. It was a time where fires were lit on which medicinal and magical herbs were burned, and through whose gusting smoke the cattle and sheep and other livestock were driven, in order that the healing and protective properties of this mystical disinfectant should go with them, out into the unfenced pastures.

Woodland Weddings

Fires also formed a traditional part of the Gypsy or Woodland Weddings which took place at this time of year. As it was considered unlucky to marry during Lent, couples had to wait until after Easter to plight their troth, and sometimes, in those days before Family Planning, the bride was already showing signs of her husband-to-be's child at the marriage feast. It was usually thought of as a good sign, showing the fertility of the couple, until the church began to frown on pregnancy outside wedlock. The old Woodland Wedding was celebrated when the couple, in the presence of their friends, chose to marry each other, for 'a year and a day'. To seal their bond, they would leap over a bonfire hand in hand.

May Day

The idea of going 'A Maying', when young people were allowed out all night to hunt through the woods and coppices for the first branches of flowering hawthorn, and bring these back to deck the houses on the one and only day this taboo plant was allowed inside the home, gave many of them the first chance to explore other aspects of human companionship, making love in the new greenery with their chosen partners, whose company they may have been denied during the winter.

One of the first trees to show its leaves is the sycamore, and it is usual in those towns and villages that still decorate their houses with greenery on May Day, especially in Cornwall, to use leafy sycamore branches as well as white hawthorn blossoms. Sycamore is the wood which is usually used to carve Love Spoons from, as it may be carved whilst still green. It is also often the leaves of sycamore which spring from the beard and mouth of the many 'Jack in the Green' or foliate heads, found in old churches and on many Victorian municipal buildings throughout the land. A tree which demonstrates both the return of life after winter, and has many associations with human love, is a beautiful symbol to have around your door.

The May Day Festival is celebrated all over Europe in a variety of ways, with dances, decorated buildings, processions of young children in bright costumes, with early flowers and merry music. In the West of England there are two celebrations which bring many of these factors together. They are experiences to be shared if you get the opportunity. The lesser, held at Minehead in North Somerset, is a procession of a strange, boat-shaped hobby horse. Appearing on the evening of 30 April to begin the festival, and then dancing through the dawn-lit streets on 1 May, this half hobby, half boat links the ancient connections between the sea-faring nature of the people with their land-based wives and families. It is supposed to be a celebration of rescuing a cow from a ship-wreck (this beribboned horse used to have a cow's tail) but it almost certainly dates back to the earlier feasts when an ox was roasted to celebrate the return of Spring.

A stranger beast yet is to be discovered at the May Day Festival in Padstow, on the North Coast of Cornwall – the 'Obby 'Oss. The creature consists of a great disc of black material, balanced on the shoulders of a stalwart dancer, surrounded by a long black skirt. His head is hidden within a black, red and white pointed mask which looks very African close up. Led by a Teaser, this strange character sways and dances through the streets of the little town, emerging at various times of day from the Golden Lion public house. There are traditional songs of praise and insult sung at all these occasions, but the strangest part of all is when the great heart-beat rhythm of the drum is stilled and the tune changes into the minor key.

> Where is St George?
> O where is he, O?
> He's out in his long-boat all on the salt sea O.
> Up flies the kite and down falls the lark O,
> There was an old woman who had an old ewe,
> And she died in her own park, O.

These words have been sung in recent years; what they may have once meant no one can be certain, but the links with that dragon slayer, St George, with boats, and with death, at the end of winter is an atmospheric moment. The great circular disc-horse sinks to the ground, and there is silence among the crowds thronging the streets, decked with flags and bunting and greenery. Then Thud, Thud, the drum picks up the beat, the black creature of wintery death regains its feet and goes on:

> Unite, and unite, let us all unite,
> For summer is a come in today,
> And whither we are going, let us all unite
> In the merry morning of May.

There are two other 'Osses at Padstow. The second is the Blue Riband Horse, founded by the Temperance Society at the end of the last century. Its members considered that the drinking of ale and cider in great quantities, not to mention the eating of vast piles of Cornish Pasties, was unseemly, so they set about producing a rival 'Oss. The third one is a miniature, and in some ways the most touching, for it is traditionally danced by the children. This introduces them gently to this ancient and magical ritual.

All seem to enjoy their day of glory and dance in the streets and around the May Pole (a tall ship's mast in the old days), which stands decorated with flowers and greenery in the town square. Groups congregate here to chat over this year and last year.

Originally, the beast of Padstow was a real black horse skin, a stallion whose interior dancer scattered dirty water to ensure fertility, now that

the power of winter was on the wane. This was replaced by the circular 'Oss, with black skirt made of tarpaulin, and fearfully heavy it is too. This used to be tarred so that young ladies swept into its ebony embrace would come forth marked with black, a sure sign of fertility to come. At the end of the nineteenth century the local vicar tried to exchange the wild fertility-orientated activities with something tamer, such as a barn dance and ox roast, but fortunately for those of us who love these ancient rites, the populace stuck with their own wild music, loud drums and black horse, and the horseplay which went with it.

The Helston Furry Dance

Still in Cornwall, on 8 May, still within that solar-powered time slot when the sun can be seen rising sequentially over the St Michael hills, Helston has its own Furry Dance. It is sometimes called 'The Floral Dance' by outsiders, who consider it to be a celebration of the Roman Goddess of Spring, 'Flora', but the locals call it the Furry Dance. The Helston Silver Band, the musicians who play for the dances, learn the music by ear from those who have played it for years. There are a number of dances following serpentine routes around the town beginning at seven in the morning. With a great thump the drummer leads off from the Town Hall, and the smartly dressed dancers, ladies and gentlemen hand in hand, sedately step through the streets. They enter various shops and houses along the way, blessing in the time-honoured fashion, with music and ceremony, everywhere they pass.

The streets here are decked with flowers and greenery. As it is held one week later than the Padstow festival, there is a little more new growth to find. At Padstow, the town's May Pole is decorated with bluebells and cowslips, but the flower of Helston is the sweet-scented lily of the valley, worn in the caps of the bandsmen, and in the lapels of the dancers in formal morning dress, who snake their way through the streets after noon. Between the morning dance and the afternoon one there are displays from representatives of all the local schools, where the white-clad children show their paces. The little girls have circlets of flowers in their hair (the type depends on which school they are from) and the small boys wear buttonholes. The leaders of these dances have to have been born in Helston; this is becoming a harder condition to fulfil, because of the closure of local maternity hospitals.

Where Padstow has something of the wildness of the upsurge of Spring power, Helston is gentle, coming in like a floodtide of growing energy, seeping through the town and spreading to the land around. Both are worth seeing, but if too many outsiders go, then the local people will be swamped. This is one of the paradoxes of such festivals. Many want to go there, making a pilgrimage to the small countryside or seaside place, to share the music, the vibrations of human energy concentrated on the welcoming of the returning power of the Sun, yet by being there they dilute the energy, and take away more than they can give to what is, after all, a local tradition.

Robin Hood

A final part of this Cornish Spring celebration is the 'Hal an Tow Play', a kind of sung Mumming Play, telling the story of the various battles between Good and Evil, and Light and Dark. Robin Hood and his merry men are there, with St George and his opposing Dragon, and St Michael, the town's patron saint, attacking the

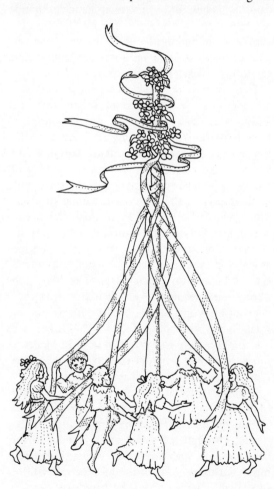

Devil. These old forces of Light are represented now by saints and heroes, but previously, and this is deeply embedded in the folk soul, they were represented by their pagan counterparts, the Gods of the Sun and Sky.

Robin Hood, partly human hero and partly spirit of the Wild Wood, is a common factor in many May Day revels. He is the green-faced foliate head, Jack in the Green, step-son of the great god Pan; he is the renewed vigour of the countryside in spring, the sun-powered cover which brushes the land with emerald and jade. He may have been a real outlaw, living in Nottingham Forest at the time of King Richard I, but he has inherited an older mantle, and at the beginning of May he turns up in his spiritual role.

In many places there is the crowning of the May Queen, traditionally a young girl, who is enthroned among her companions, and perhaps escorted by a May King, or in many places, Robin Hood and his Merry Men. She is a modern version of Maid Marian, the ancient White Lady who could change herself into a deer to hide in the forest, who brought healing water from the secret springs, and who cared for all the wild creatures, the birds and the forest itself.

May Poles and Dowsing

Another frequent aspect of these celebrations is May Pole dancing, a widespread tradition found all over the country and now, fortunately, being recovered. May Poles used to stand on the village green of many places, but during the purges of the Reformation, when any kind of singing and dancing was frowned upon, and all old traditions, whether they smacked of Popery or paganism, were repressed, these symbols of life, linking the reviving energy of the Sky with the living matter of the growing Earth beneath, were pulled down. The binding with ribbons and circling dance steps represent the eternal tidal patterns of energy being sent down from the Sun, and then the unwinding shows how, through the spreading growth of plants and all that feed on them, the power is returned to the sky in a cyclic and unending pattern.

Dowsers, whose sensitivity is increased by the

use of dowsing rods, either of traditional hazel or willow, or in these days of high tech, of copper or steel, have detected the spiral patterns created in places where there is, or used to be, a May Pole. They have also sensed the wide bands of flowing energy which seem to cross and weave about the May Day sunrise line, making a kind of double helix, so like the form of entwined DNA in all living cells.

Dowsing is an art nearly everyone can master, and whatever one's scientific outlook, it can show subtle flows of energy around sacred places, or even the natural patterns of underground water, or beneficial influences which seem to emanate from traditionally blessed or holy sites. Make a pendulum out of a small weight and a piece of thin string and hold it over your free hand. Ask it to make a swing to indicate 'yes', or ask 'Is my name ...?' whatever it happens to be, and when you have got a movement that is clear, ask a question to which the answer is 'no', and the movement should change direction. That is the basic art.

You may then be able to find the edges of areas where old dances took place by mentally saying to yourself 'Is this the edge of the dancing ground?' and moving in a straight line towards the centre, or a May Pole, or other old mark stone. Most people, given a bit of patience and practice, can get this to work.

May Flowers

May is a time when garden roses come into bloom, as do some of the glorious lilies which are being grown more widely now. These two familiar flowers have very old roots; they are often depicted in early churches, or carved as pew ends or column capitals, or shown in the stained glass of the windows. The rose is a very important symbol, similar to the lotus blossom in the sacred art of India and Egypt. It represents the flowering of the spiritual dimension of the human soul, from its secret closed-up state in most people, to the sparkling golden centre revealed in those who have awoken to the marvel that there is more to life than most people are able to see.

The image of the rose has long been used in religious art, often as a symbol of the Virgin Mary, as has the lily, and both are important in the ancient arts of alchemy. Each shows transformation, from the green and earthy bud to the open flower with its velvet petals of red or white. The poetic references to both flowers show how their shining forms have influenced those inspired and light-spirited ones through the ages. We too may be similarly inspired, if we are able to really look at these summer blooms, and see them with more than ordinary eyes.

May Garlands form another small aspect of this widely celebrated festival time. Sometimes they are mere posies of flowers on a pole, but on occasion they can be quite elaborate flower-decked spheres, made of three interlocking circles of cane or wire and covered with whatever wild and cultivated blossoms the area produces. This may be carried by a group in fancy dress, including a May Queen and a Green Man, who is sometimes himself completely covered by a framework of branches, beribboned and decked with flowers. He is probably a survival of that earlier Green Man, who was woven from leafy fronds and cast into the sea or onto a bonfire as part of an ancient sacrifice, or as a form of blessing. The Roman writers alleged that the Celts sacrificed people inside huge wicker figures, but it is rather unlikely as wood would burn quickly and release the captives. It is more likely that shapes of men and animals were woven of branches and leaves, and it was these which were burned, perhaps with something tasty being barbecued at the same time to provide a feast.

Sacred Trees

The raising of a Sacred Tree is a widespread and ancient form of celebration. In Scandinavia it was often a birch tree, with the branches removed, which was taken to a special place in the village and decked with ribbons and real or paper flowers, in memory of *Yggdrasil*, the World Tree around which all creation centred. In some places the May Pole was a new tree cut each year and in others one which lasted fifteen to twenty years, often painted red and white. Near the sea it was often a ship's mast, so it was a company of sailors who had the task of raising the pole, with windlasses and ropes if it was very tall. One set up in London was over 130 feet tall and took twelve men half a day to get it upright.

Decorating trees or branches or the tying of rags or ribbons to living trees as a small offering is an ancient rite, still found in parts of Cornwall and Ireland. This was also done as a request for healing, or for protection on a journey or for the return of a loved one. Pins, too, were a suitable small price to pay a water spirit or well-spring fairy for a bit of luck, and after being held between the hands whilst the request was silently made they were stuck into the bark of the healing tree or cast into the waters of the holy well. Iron nails and knives were used to ward off harm, and if someone was thought to have used evil spells to harm your household or livestock you would have to creep up behind them and pin their shadow to the ground with any iron instrument, even crossed scissor blades, to break the spell and heal the sick. It is for this reason that an iron horse shoe is lucky, for it has seven nails, a lucky number, and when fixed upright becomes a symbol of the Holy Grail, or the Cup of Good Luck. Only working farriers may nail their horseshoes upside down, for they have magical control over the iron they shape, and don't need the extra luck.

Oak Apple Day

Towards the end of May there is a festival commemorating the Restoration of the Monarchy in 1660 when Charles II returned to London. It is also called Oak Apple Day, because after the Battle of Worcester in 1651 the king hid in an oak tree. People used to wear the gilded oak galls or 'apples' and chase those who were not so Royalist in their outlook with bunches of stinging nettles. This is not so common a custom now, although in some places churches or houses are still dressed with greenery, particularly oak leaves, if any can be found at this time of year.

There is also at this time a celebration of the people's rights to cut wood in the forests. At Wishford Magna in Wiltshire it is traditional that a great branch or tree be cut, by hand, then carried through the village to cries of 'Grovely! Grovely! Grovely! And all Grovely! Unity is strength!' Some branches are even taken to Salisbury Cathedral in memory of this ancient ritual, which probably confirms the common people's right to cut wood for their fires, or to use about their holdings. This is also done in other places, such as Epping Forest, both at the beginning of May, and at the end of summer at Hallowe'en. Both dates are ancient Fire Festivals in the Celtic calendar.

Flower Festivals

May is also the month of the Chelsea Flower Show, a great festival for flower growers, gardeners and horticulturists throughout the land, to show their prize blooms, arrangements, or new specimens to a delighted audience. Held in the grounds of the Royal Hospital, home of the Chelsea Pensioners, gardens are built and marquees set up full of prize flowers, plants, cacti and all manner of wonderful greenery, from all round the world.

Another flowery ceremony is that of the lilies and roses, placed in the Wakefield Tower at the Tower of London around 21 May, to commemorate the death of Henry VI, who was murdered there. The red roses come from the Kings College, Cambridge, and the lilies, bound with pale blue silk, from Eton College. This has happened every year since 1923, when a marble slab to record his death was placed in the Tower. A simple prayer in Latin, composed by Henry VI, is read at the time of placing the memorial bouquet.

With the new abundance of flowers, bees may be swarming, and are worth taking.

A swarm of bees in May is worth a load of hay.
A swarm of bees in June is worth a silver spoon.
A swarm of bees in July is only worth a fly!

In the countryside, May was always considered a time of plenty, especially as far as dairy products go. The Anglo-Saxon name for the month was 'Thrimilci', the time when cows gave so much milk that they had to be milked three times a day. Butter, cheese and cream were all plentiful too.

TAURUS, THE BULL

In May not only are people appreciating the flowers of parks and gardens but animals, both wild and tame, must prefer the warmer weather, the new spring grass and the leafy greenery all round. This is the time of the zodiacal sign of Taurus, the Bull, an animal with a very long history of ceremonial connections, both as an offering of meat at feast days, and as an animal of strength and traction, for ox power ruled the land for many centuries. Those born between about 21 April to 20 May come under the Sign of Taurus, which is ruled by the planet Venus, she who governs love, partnerships, beauty and peace. Taureans are often gentle, lazy and easy-going people, loving the good things in life – fine food, intelligent company and beautiful sur-roundings. Being country folk at heart, they make excellent hosts, reliable friends and pleasant companions, although, like any bull, or cow in defence of her calf, a Taurean can be fierce and determined.

Those born in the first half of May will have a great love for all things beautiful music, possessions, people, gardens. They will have a great sense of appreciation for the good things in life, particularly food and wine. Many are excellent cooks, turning the fresh vegetables and herbs from their garden into enjoyable meals, perhaps decorated with flowers and set out among sparkling glasses and silverware. They often delight in intimate dinners where they are able to demonstrate their talents to a few chosen friends.

Taureans tend to be of shorter stature, and, if they over-do the wining and dining, it will show up in their figures. As children they tend to be chunky, with curly hair, often dark. Some can become spotty as teenagers, and show shyness and withdrawal because of their complexions, but they do grow out of this phase.

Making excellent and loving partners, though growing into their relationships and business connections slowly, they may be annoyed if hurried, and be critical or pernickety over details. They may suffer from throat complaints, including glandular or other conditions affecting their voices. They may also be 'a pain in the neck', or suffer from stiffness or muscular cramps there. Many women with Taurus prominent in their charts have very long and elegant necks, which look particularly beautiful, when garlanded with the blues and greens of sapphires, emeralds, turquoise, lapis lazuli and green moss agates.

The plants for this month include many already mentioned in this chapter, roses, lilies, both of the valley and the madonna ones, as well as violets, bluebells and daisies. The early leafing sycamore is also a tree associated with Taurus, and Venus, the planet which rules this sign. Most Taureans look well in all shades of blue and green, but should keep clear of bright red, although more muted shades of rose pink or salmon might suit quite well.

MAY RECIPES

Cornish Pasty

1 lb/500g/2 cups diced rump steak
2 potatoes, diced
2 onions, chopped
1 turnip, diced
2 tbsp beef stock
1 lb/500g/2 cups shortcrust pastry
1 egg, beaten

Mix together the beef, potatoes, onions and turnip. Add the stock and season with salt and pepper. Roll out the dough thinly and cut into four circles. Put one quarter of the filling on one half of each circle. Dampen the dough edges with water and bring the empty half over to cover the filling, sealing the edges of dough to form a semi-circle. Flute the edges with your fingers. Lay the pasties on a lightly greased baking sheet and brush with the beaten egg. Bake in a preheated 425°F/220°C/Mark 7 oven for 15 to 20 minutes, or until golden brown. Then reduce the oven temperature to 350°F/180°C/Mark 4 and bake for a further 20 minutes.

Spring Posy Chocolate Mousse

1 lb/500g/2⅓ cups dark chocolate, broken
  into pieces
8 eggs, separated
3 tbsp brandy
chocolate granules
a few fresh spring flowers as available

Melt the chocolate over hot water. Add a drop of water if it is too thick, and stir to keep it smooth. Stir the egg yolks into the chocolate mixture. Beat the egg whites until very stiff. Fold the brandy into the chocolate and egg mixture and then fold in the egg whites. Pour the mixture into small, tumbler-shaped glasses. Leave the mousses to set in a cool place.

To serve, sprinkle the top of each glass with some chocolate granules. Wrap the stems of small bunches of spring flowers, with leaves, in silver foil, and push a posy gently into the top of each mousse.

May Day Cake

A May Day cake, made of Victoria sponge, topped with buttercream icing and decorated with a May Pole and hawthorn blossoms, makes a festive tea for the May Queen and her retinue.

Victoria sponge
6 oz/175g/¾ cup margarine
6 oz/175g/¾ cup caster sugar
6 oz/175g/1½ cups plain flour
pinch bicarbonate of soda
1 tsp baking powder
3 eggs, well beaten
2 tbsp warm water

Buttercream icing
4 oz/125g/½ cup butter, softened
6 oz/175g/1⅓ cups sifted icing sugar
2 tbsp lemon juice
few drops pink food colouring (optional)

To finish
2 tbsp apricot jam
barleysugar or candy stick
ribbons or strands of wool
a few May blossoms

To make the cake, cream together the margarine and sugar, then add the flour, bicarbonate of soda and the baking powder. Slowly beat in the eggs and water. Grease two round sponge tins and cook at 450°F/220°/Mark 7 for 20 minutes. Cool the cakes on a rack.

For the icing, beat together the butter and sugar, with a little pink colouring if you like.

When the cakes are cool, cover the top of one with the jam and place the other cake on top. Coat the top and sides with the buttercream icing. Make a May Pole with the barleysugar or candy stick and streamers of ribbon or wool. Stick this into the centre of the cake with the streamers spread out and hanging over the edge. Decorate the platter with the May Blossoms or pink and white flowers.

A PLAY PAVILION TO MAKE

This is a simple and effective way to make a small tent or pavilion for children either in the garden as shelter from rain as the May Queen's Bower, or as a Fortune Teller's Tent for a summer fête, or even the Witches Cave, indoors for Hallowe'en. All you need is a Garden Umbrella on its stand, perhaps a bit lower than you would use it for adults, a length of rope about the same length as the circumference of the opened umbrella, and some old curtains or a sheet long enough to reach the ground, and be weighted down, and wide enough to go right round the circum-ference of the umbrella easily. Put up the umbrella, being sure it is secure, then thread or pin the curtains or sheet on the rope, tying the ends firmly together. Make the curtains into a 'skirt' right round the umbrella and fix the edges with weights, pulling them out a bit.

The curtains may be decorated with real vines and flowers for the May Queen, or cut-out shapes to match the purpose or season, such as spooky shapes for the Hallowe'en Party. A small chair or stool and a mat for the floor will be all that is needed to make this a delightful bower for the Festival.

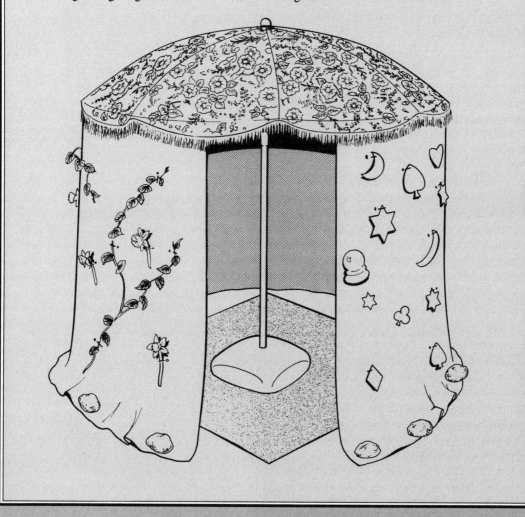

MAY SONG

Here We Come Gathering Nuts In May

Here we come gathering nuts in May,
Nuts in May, yes, nuts in May;
Here we come gathering nuts in May
On a cold and frosty morning.

And whom will you take for nuts in May?

We'll take *Jane Brown* for nuts in May.

Whom will you send to fetch her away?

We'll send *Martin Smith* to fetch her
away.

Originally it was 'Here we go gathering KNOTS of
May ...' a knot being a posy of flowers which were
brought into the house. May the First was the only
day of the year that the taboo against these knots
could be broken.

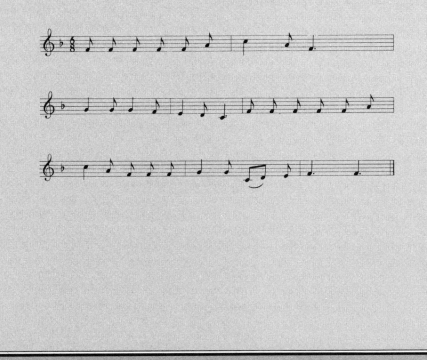

JUNE

Then doth the joyful feast of St John the Baptist
take his turn,
When bonfires great with lofty flame, in every
town do burn;
And young men round with maids, do dance in
every street,
With garlands wrought of Motherwort, or else
with Vervain sweet.

Thomas Kirchmeyer: *The Joyful Feast of St John*

(sixteenth century)

June is often still only the promise of summer, and though Midsummer's Day falls here, it is not usually in the middle of the hottest time; nor is June the most relaxed of the months. The long light evenings caused the old agricultural labourers heavy work in the hay fields, cutting, tedding and stacking the hay on which their livestock would survive the winter. Dry days which ensured the hay was properly cured might well have followed hard on the heels of the sheep dipping and shearing. All around crops needed tending, weeding or garnering for the table. Anxious eyes would be watching for infestations of birds or pests, or drought, for it is during the long lighted June days that crops of corn would begin to fill out, and many other green harvests would begin to show their promise.

To schoolchildren June is often a time of torment, when perhaps suffering from 'hay fever' and pollen allergies they have to struggle through very important examinations or tests at the end of the school year. When the warm sun beckons, and the pleasant, star-lit evenings encourage all to linger in the scented twilight, it is dreadful to be incarcerated in classrooms or lecture halls, grabbing those last few facts which might make the difference between a pass and a failure.

Now many of the older, simpler herbal remedies are being re-examined for their power against many of the ills we civilised folk endure. June was a time of gathering both wild and cultivated herbal plants and shrubs, drying them in the warm air, and storing them safe for later use. Some, of course, like all the culinary herbs, are used green; in salads, both sweet and savoury, and in many simple dishes, like omelettes with mixed herbs, yogurt dishes with mint and parsley, cream cheese with chives and garlic stuffed

into barbecued roast potatoes. Also to be enjoyed is all the sweet goodness of the soft fruits, so welcome at this time of year.

Strawberries and cream conjure up the whole summer experience, whether eaten as you watch the Tennis Championships at Wimbledon, or shared in a riverside picnic at Henley, or simply picked from your own garden or a nearby farm. There can be no greater pleasure than the taste of freshly picked berries, gathered by your own hand, and eaten before their clustered leaves have had a moment to wilt. Raspberries and all the currants, great green and red gooseberries, logan-berries – all those scarlet jewels of delicious sunlight – are best eaten raw or made into crim-son summer puddings veiled in cream. These must be enjoyed for the moment, as they used to be, eaten only when the fruits are in season, not frozen, preserved for some later, winter, oc-casion. That is the joy of the turning seasons; an instant sacrament of living sweetness, taken at the ripe moment, shared with those you love, in immediate and eternal celebration of the powers of life. Try to sense this simple, private moment of connection with the turning Earth, the chang-ing days, the passing harvest of so temporary a bounty. Save up the memories of summer scents, of fruits and flowers, to illuminate the dark of winter nights. Then when the artificial, frozen cherry tart comes round, awaken all those hoarded summer days, with honey sweetness in the mind and tongue, and revel in your inner hidden hoard of freshness and repletion.

Whitsuntide

Seven weeks after Easter comes Whitsuntide, a festival of outdoor games, and celebrations of the fullness of life. Taking its name from two sources, 'Wit' and 'White', it is another Church feast which spilled over to become a celebration with Whitsuntide Ales among the common folk. Pentecost, the other name of this festival, was always a time of gatherings, and returning, albeit briefly, to homes or people's manors; and many of the knights from King Arthur's court set off to begin the great quests, including the ongoing search for the Holy Grail, at this time.

Tradition has it that at Pentecost, as Jesus's disciples gathered, the Holy Spirit descended upon them giving them the prophetic tongue of wisdom, or 'wit'. From then they set off on their ministries to other peoples. Another version has it that this was 'White Sunday' when penitents or converts, dressed in white, came for baptism or absolution, originally from the Apostles and later from the Christian priesthood, around this time of year.

Morris Men

White is not only the colour of Christianity; it was always, long before that doctrine arrived in Britain, the colour of the White Goddess, the Earth Mother in her gown of daisies and Queen Anne's Lace. It is in her honour that the Morris

Men don their white garb, and deck their hats with flowers, and dance the union of sky and earth, of growing things and the successful hunt, and the unforgotten weather magic. It very seldom rains on real Morris Men! Their bells and ribbons banish harm and bring fertility; and their ribald songs (sung not when they are dancing but quaffing their fair share of Whitsun Ales) and the old practice of the cake carried spitted on a sword

to be apportioned to those around, bring traditional magic to our lives.

In many places during June there are great gatherings of these traditional dancers, at Morris Ring meetings. A notable meeting place is Thaxted in Essex. Here, dancer sides from all over the country come to show their paces, dance with sticks, with handkerchiefs, with rapper and with long swords, with light steps and with clogs, demonstrating their skills, and reaffirming the ancient art of dancing as a ritual celebration. Today there are even ladies who have taken up this once all-male preserve. Some traditionalists shudder at the sight of twirling skirts and bouncing bosoms, tripping their way through the old steps. Morris was a male tradition, danced for the White Goddess, Maryam, Marah, or Mary, and the women had secret, moon-led dances, with their domestic instruments, with sieves, and baskets, with distaffs and shawls; but these have been forgotten, except in far memory, wherein nothing is forgotten. One day these dances will

be rediscovered to take their rightful place alongside the Morris Men's dances, as a reborn part of our folk heritage.

As well as the Morris dances with short sticks of wood, which seem to represent agricultural activities such as ploughing or seed sowing; or dances of 'weather magic' when the waving white handkerchiefs might help waft away rain-bearing clouds, there are two sorts of sword dance. Long sword and rapper sword are both slower dances, and because some of them link the dancers together with their swords, elegant interwoven patterns of both people and then swords may be made. The symbol of the English Folk Dance and Song Society is a representation of six interlocked swords in the six-pointed star design. This is a very ancient magical symbol, representing the interaction of the downward pointing triangle of Sky energy fusing with the upward thrusting triangle of Earth power. It is a Western form of the Eastern *Yin-Yang* symbol, perfect harmony of masculine and feminine forces, eternally dancing in the creation of life.

Only five swords are interlinked in one tradition, making the pentagram symbol, or holy star, often seen in church windows, and carved as a mason's mark on stonework. Sometimes the Fool, usually the best dancer in any Morris side, sticks his head through the sword lock, which is suddenly broken apart, symbolically beheading him. This is an imitation of the rituals of sacrifice, when a chosen victim danced to death, as in the ballet by Stravinsky, 'The Rite of Spring', or when some animal was killed to form the main dish of the ceremonial feast, served when the dancing was done. To modern eyes this seems an archaic and cruel ritual, yet we still eat the flesh of animals killed in abattoirs, and our summer barbecues have steaks and chops on the grills, just as our Christmas table groans under the weight of a turkey.

Many Morris sides also have a Hobby Horse or totem animal as part of their team. These may take many forms, from the Horse and Rider, in which the head and body of the rider sticks up through a horse's body with a caparison round it, hiding the rider's legs, or there is a tall animal mask, with its head above that of the dancer, and a cloth covering his own shoulders and body. These Hobby Animals may take all kinds of forms, from the Westminster Men's beautiful Unicorn, to stags, (sometimes made out of a real stuffed stag's head with antlers), or bulls, or a horse's head rebuilt over a real skull, for the horse is a sacred image throughout European folk culture. There are Giants too, although the really huge ones are no longer seen in Britain. There are various Dragons and semi-mythical creatures, like the Dorset Ooser, a horned and masked human face, but the most common is probably the horse. Many of these creatures have hinged jaws so that they can snap at the audience, or be used to collect money in their mouths to pay for the beer, or for a local charity.

Where Morris dances meet Mumming Plays there is a cross over of some of the characters. In some Morris dances there is a Fool or Man/Woman, sometimes called 'Betty' or 'The Betty', or the Fool is dressed in women's clothes (even though he sports a beautiful beard or moustache) and may have a padded front or fake breasts to fill out his costume. This character is another traditional reminder of the cross-dressed priests of many religions, both ancient and modern. Men in skirts have served a mystical purpose for hundreds of years. Priests of many ancient traditions wore the dresses and sometimes hairstyles of women, and today modern vicars and bishops retain the long skirts of their order, and judges and barristers wear elaborate wigs.

A bishop's mitre is a representation of the fish-headed god of the ancient Sumerians, yet another reminder of the link between animal heads and deities, brought to a complex pantheon among the ancient Egyptians. Visitors to the ruined temples there see many fine examples of the Mother Goddess, Hathor, shown with the head of a cow; Horus, the Sun God, depicted as a hawk; Anubis, the Guardian God with the dog-like jackal head, and Osiris, lord of the fertility of the Nile with a green face, like our own Jack in the Green, or Robin Goodfellow.

Sacred dancers from the Andes to the Himalayas share the white costume, the bells and bright ribbons, and a musical accompaniment from a small band of local instrument players. In places where the Christian faith has made an impact, the ceremonial dances are often carried out on the feast days of the Virgin Mary, or of other female saints, and sometimes the image of this Holy Lady is carried in procession from her shrine around the town or village.

Many of the Morris Ring meetings, which bring together dancers from all the traditions of this popular form of folk ceremony, begin their day of dancing in the local church, and it is hard to tell if the blessing flows from the Christian priest to the dancers, or from the celebrants of the ancient rites of luck and fertility to the church. David may have danced before the Lord in the Bible but, apart from some of the imported or charismatic churches, dancing before the altar is a fairly rare sight these days. Dancing in churchyards used to be an important occasion for all the parishioners, at Harvest and Seed Time, at weddings and perhaps, in the early days, at wakes, for many ancient churches occupy the same space or physical high place that an earlier sacred centre stood upon. You can often detect this very old foundation by the fact that the church yard is

circular, or that there are massive stones set in its walls, which may have previously been part of a pattern of standing stones. Any dowser would be able to detect the energy which still exists in such solar markers, and some of them can be felt to tingle, or give off warmth to the hand of an investigator. Celtic crosses, old burial mounds and sacred wells beside the church are sure signs that they have inherited more than a central place in the hearts of their congregations!

Miracle Plays

In some places, as well as the revival of dances, there is a new interest in the old Miracle Plays, often performed out of doors in good weather. The time around Whitsun, when Easter is late in a particular year, brings forth a number of such performances. Coming somewhere in between the real theatrical performances, which have only occupied actual theatre buildings since the latter half of the sixteenth century, and the religious enactments of parts of the Bible by Craftsmen's Guilds, they tell parts of an ongoing cycle of the Creation of the World. In more down-to-earth ways, the Mumming Plays, with characters such as Saint George or King George, the Moorish/

Turkish Knight with his black face, and the Magician/Doctor whose mysterious draught restores those slain to life, reflect the ancient pattern of life, growth, death and rebirth.

Midsummer Bonfires

At Midsummer, St John's Eve, or the Longest Day, which all fall between 21 and 24 June, there has been a very old tradition of lighting bonfires on beacon hills, especially in Cornwall and the West Country, where many such high points dot the landscape. The original idea was to both celebrate the power of the Sun at his zenith and implore him not to wane and withdraw into the cold and dark of winter. If enough bonfires were lit on enough hilltops it was considered that a net of flame-light would lie over the land, and strengthen the Sun. Processions of people with flaming torches would circle their fields, bare after the hay had been cut, and still green with growing corn, marking their boundaries and blessing their land with light, song, mimes of reaping and harvest dances. Now, as earlier in the year, the people decked their houses and their clothes with garlands of wild flowers, and in the waning twilight, climbed to the top of the local high point, bearing dry wood or branches.

In many places in Cornwall these same beacon hills flame with wind-torn firelight, and the scent of woodsmoke drifts across the valleys. Often nowadays the local brass or silver band is in attendance, and they hump their shining instruments up the steep and winding paths, in the damp or sultry evening. Often the parish priest comes along too, and in some places a Harvest Mother or Earth Lady with a gang of flower-dressed supporters, harking back to the blithe days of the May revels, or the merry years of pagan rites. She carries a posy of flowers, some garden ones or herbs, nine valuable plants, and also nine weeds, to cast into the flames. Here and there, where customs die hardest, an ancient blessing is spoken in the tongue of this Western Land, in Cornish, as well as English, asking a blessing on the beneficial crops and a curse of fire upon the weeds. Once her bouquet has been assigned to the pyre the flames start to leap up, the band strikes up hymns or perhaps more popular tunes, and those with the energy or inclination may dance about the bonfire, as did their forefathers in the ages past. There is much old magic here, from the selecting of the herbs and weeds, to the ceremonial binding with five coloured ribbons, red and blue, green and yellow and white, uniting land and sky, summer and winter, water and fire between them.

The Glastonbury Procession

Processions of a more Christian aspect take place in many other places, and at Glastonbury there is a great gathering around midsummer, when clergy and choirs from all over the country make pilgrimage to the 'Holyest Earthe in England' as it was once called. Here, according to legend, came Joseph of Arimathea bearing the sacred cruets with the blood and sweat of Christ and here, beneath the skewed Tor's shadow, he made the first simple chapel, dedicated to Mary the Virgin, Mother of God. On a hillside nearby, pausing in his journey, he struck his hawthorn staff into the fertile soil and it sprouted, and to this day its offspring, a species of foreign hawthorn, blooms twice each year. The first flowering is around Epiphany, Old Christmas or 6 January, when a flowering sprig is still delivered to the Queen; and the second flowering is alongside the other hawthorns, early in May.

Now this pilgrimage draws together many fervent Christians to walk these holy hills and sacred vales, and in their own way reaffirm the ancient contact with their church's roots in Britain. Hymns are sung, and the main street of this seemingly dull little market town in Somerset is packed with bright banners and the wafting scent of incense, which is uncommon in the Church of England except at such festive gatherings. Choirs sing and wend their long processional way, in the scarlets, blues, blacks and purples of their sacerdotal garb. Splendid priests in snowy linen, bedecked with the finest embroidery their parish can provide, stride proudly at the heads of their own parishioners, from St John's Church to the Abbey, which was once the greatest church in Britain but is now blackbird-haunted ruins, thanks to Henry VIII. The glory may have departed from this great church, but the shadowed masonry reflects an ancient power, which hovers like a blessing mist in the undercroft chapel.

Pilgrimages

Summer was always a time of pilgrimage, long before the Industrial Revolution brought the idea of holidays to their hardpressed workers. Holy Days and Holy places linked many a medieval traveller, to whom the walk to Jerusalem, City of Peace, was not too long, if their faith was strong enough. We, who are used to the speed of jets and instant, worldwide communication, perhaps feel we have a monopoly on long-distance travel, yet our ancestors, in pursuit of wars or religious impulses often walked, rode on horseback or travelled on carts hundreds or thousands of miles during their lifetimes. When it was fashionable to visit certain shrines, dedicated to particular saints, or places where significant sacred events took place, people flocked in their thousands, seeking absolution or benediction from their travails. Even now folk make long and painful journeys to the shrine of St Bernadette at Lourdes, or our own Walsingham or, if their spirit for healing is prompted by older views, to the hot spring of Aquae Sulis, at Bath.

Pilgrimage is one of those forgotten words, yet in our hearts many of us long to be present at some crucial moment to seek comfort or blessing by simply being there. Today these trips are more often made to Pop Concerts or vast charity events, when the music is just a unifying factor allowing people of different cultures to share a time and place. In earlier times, it was the longing to be present at the hill from which a saint left the earth, or at a well or river where the baptisms took place. The old Green Roads of Britain provided a long, figure-of-eight route, known to some as 'the Gypsy Switch', along which traders, hawkers and pilgrims wandered, in the warmer months, seeking a living from craftswork, or salvation from their act of piety. Many of us still have that inner yearning, yet cannot identify the cause. It may well be the same for today's travellers, who may not have Romany blood in their veins, but who share the longing for perpetual travel, for wandering the green roads, resting briefly here and there. Nowadays this is met with prohibition in an ordered world. When such travellers try to gather to make music, sell their wares and exchange ideas and information, as they used to be able to do at many Free Fairs about the countryside, they are harrassed, and driven on. Their plight is not new, nor is the wandering urge which drives them from settled homes to roost in vans without the merest necessities of life, which we rooted house dwellers take for granted.

Stonehenge

Stonehenge, in recent years, has become a philosophical – and sometimes literal – battleground. A few decades ago only a handful of Neo-Druids, their supporters, and people awake after all-night parties at midsummer, came to see the sun rise

over the Hele Stone, and see it cast its fertilising shadow into the centre of the circle of small, alien bluestones, brought there from the Prescelli Mountains. There, there was a conjunction of the ancient solar Temple, with its accurately aligned marking stones and slots between, where

the equinoctial and solstitial sun made its entry to the ring. Some people have an inner urge to pilgrimage to experience this. It has been a moment of great power, when in a small, unmilitary company, in dawn's dim light, the scarlet rising sun pauses a sacred moment upon the Hele Stone, before arcing its way into the azure vault of heaven. At that instant is a great upwelling of feeling, linking the modern technological mind with those who mastered stone and earth and sacred geometry so many thousand years ago to create this massive, massy sundial on Salisbury Plain. It is the Giant's Dance, the Hedge of Stones, the Sphere of Light Greek poets wrote about. If that is not a solar, souler magnet even in this frantic world, I don't know what might be.

The modern Druid Order, which has recently been driven out from this place given to the Nation in perpetuity, alongside the vast crowds which try to gather for a music festival nearby, may not have very ancient roots, but its forebearers certainly had a knowledge of the starry wisdom, and the power of Sun and Moon, those Gods uncreated by human minds. They may not have been the builders of such vast and airy Temples to the sky as Stonehenge, Avebury, Arbor Low and Stanton Drew, Castlerigg and Callenish, yet they seemed to hold such places as sacrosanct, according to disparaging Roman accounts. Those ancient sites were constructed over hundreds of years, between about 3,000 BC and 1,500 BC, involving vast amounts of earth and rock shifting with no more than the shoulderblade of a red deer and a woven basket. Some of the stones that were moved and set up weigh over fifty tons, and where there are interlocking lintels, these fit exactly, both the pegs at the tops of the uprights, and the curve of the circle. Given modern tools and equipment such an achievement would be hard; using nothing more than measuring sticks and hard rock to shape the sarsens (saracen, or foreign stones) and the will and intelligence to set out a pattern exactly, over hundreds of years, it was an enormous task. There must have been some religious impulse underlying the effort, which humbles modern constructions.

GEMINI, THE TWINS

Those whose birthdays fall between 21 May and about 21 June come under the sign of Gemini, the Twins. Geminians' nature is often a dual one. They sometimes have two very different sets of friends; for example, those concerned with work, and those met through hobbies. Gemini folk are clever, quick witted, and their ruling planet is Mercury, the communicator in the sky. They can be enthusiastic and charming, but they can sometimes change, to show the reverse of their sunny nature, which is secretive or unapproachable. They can be very open-handed and generous, and then without seeming to have taken offence, at the next meeting they can be tight-fisted and mean. To say they are two-faced is both true and uncomplimentary; those who know them well will probably have experienced both aspects of their twin nature.

Gemini people include such volatile and expansive names as William Pitt, mathematician; Blaise Pascal and George Stephenson; but writers and poets also come from this intelligent and communicative sign, and they include Thomas Hardy, Walt Whitman, Charles Kingsley, the Russian poet Pushkin, and Lord Lytton. Today they are often well known in the field of hi-tech and computer systems, because their sharp intellect and quick thinking can help them develop new systems and programs.

The sign under which you were born is not the only influencing factor, of course; the position of other planets on your natal day have a bearing, too. The position of the Moon can influence a person's nature, and the interrelationship of all the planets in a horoscope has to be taken into account when an astrologer is trying to discover a person's hidden talents and abilities and the areas of their lives in which there could be difficulties. Geminians, being under a twin sign, some-

times have a darker side to their characters. Their ruling planet is Mercury, who as well as looking after transport, communications and inventiveness is also concerned with thievery, scheming and underhand dealings, which Geminians can carry out with the sweetest smiles on their faces.

The busy lifestyles of Gemini people can lead them to suffer from mental strain and anxiety, especially if they are trying to push a doubtful deal through, but it can also affect their hands and arms, being especially unpleasant for many of them who have to work keyboards or construct delicate things with their hands. They can also get very agitated or irritable if their plans are thwarted, and it is a good idea for them to take up a relaxing hobby, such as walking in the country, one involving travel, or growing special plants or herbs, for example, which will attract their eye for detail.

The colours which suit them best include shades of amber and yellow, light green, and they look very good in silvery greys, white and the opal colours which are sometimes fashionable. Dark, heavy or bright colours make them look pale. As they are given to travelling a lot, for both work and play, sets of expensive matching luggage, or an unusual handbag or briefcase may well be among their most treasured possessions. The jewels they like will reflect the colours and include amber, jade and diamonds (whose sparkle may attract some of their desires to embezzle). The texture and forms of semiprecious stones please them too. Especially liked are various agates, chrysoprase, and pale peridots. They are also drawn by the silvery settings of platinum, reflecting the quicksilver of Mercury, and perhaps some styles of modern jewellery made of aluminium or titanium, especially if set with opaline colours.

Okrochka (Cold Soup)

2 cartons yogurt
milk, same volume as yogurt
4 oz/125g/1 cup diced fresh cucumber
3 oz/90g/½ cup chopped pickled cucumber
or gherkin
4 oz/125g/½ cup diced cooked chicken
finely chopped fennel leaves to taste
salt and pepper
2 hard-boiled eggs

Mix the yogurt and milk in a large bowl and stir in all the other ingredients. Other herbs may be added, such as mint, parsley and chives, but not enough to cover up the fennel flavour. Add salt and fresh ground pepper and chill the soup in the fridge for two hours or more. Before serving, chop the hard-boiled eggs and add them to the soup, with a sprinkle of herbs and black pepper on top.

Gooseberry Sorbet

1½ lb/625g gooseberries
8 oz/250g sugar
1 pint/60cl water
1 egg white
juice of one lemon
few drops of green food colouring (optional)

Wash, then top and tail gooseberries. Simmer with the water and sugar until soft. Strain through a sieve and add the lemon juice and colouring. Cool, then put into an ice tray and freeze for about one hour. At this point the sorbet should be partially frozen. Stir it well, fold in the well-beaten egg white and return to the freezer for two hours.

Refreshing sorbets can be made not only from many summer fruits, such as strawberries, raspberries and blackcurrants, but also from fragrant flowers, such as elderflowers, and from fragrant leaves such as young blackcurrant leaves, mint leaves and the leaves of scented geraniums. The flowers or leaves are boiled with the sugar and water then left to steep until the mixture is cool. They are then strained off before the syrup is frozen.

Elderflower Champagne

One of the generally ignored riches of June are white elderflowers, common in country lanes and often growing beside abandoned houses. The flavour of these delicate, creamy flowers is unmatched. They make excellent champagne with a natural sparkle.

seven heads of elderflowers
8 pints/5 litres/10 US pints cold water
1¼ lb/600g/2½ cups sugar
2 lemons, sliced
2 tbsp white wine vinegar

Pick the flowers on a dry day when the first few flowers are falling. Bring the water to the boil and add the sugar, stirring to dissolve. Allow to cool then add the flowerheads, sliced lemon and the wine vinegar. Cover the champagne and leave it to stand for 24 hours. Syphon it off and bottle in beer bottles, so that the natural fizz can develop.

Other Uses for Elderflowers

Elderflowers may also be made into fritters. Dip the freshly picked but dry heads into a thin batter mix and fry them very quickly in hot, clean oil. Dust the fritters with caster sugar and serve as a special dessert.

Elderflowers are also delicious combined with gooseberries: try them together in pies, tarts, jams and preserves. Use just the flowers and not too much stem or stalk. The flowers can be stripped off with a fork, like blackcurrants.

JULY

Full bellied summer, hazy days, warm showers and a lambent moon,
Red fields of poppies, rainbow gardens, velvet lawns and sultry noon,
Rich fruiting orchards, shadowed glades, soft evenings when the wind is still
All these are England, bountiful and full, when July roses crowd my windowsill.

Marian Green: *Summer words*

July is another holiday month, filled with church fêtes, village gatherings, smoky barbecues, breaking-up from school, and freedom. In many places travelling fairs set down in these long and humid summer days; and we who are too used to supermarkets forget that long ago shops came to visit places, not the populace turning out to go to the shops. Hucksters and pedlars, hawkers and tinkers carried their stock or their trade on their backs, or the broader, slower ones of pack ponies or mules. From village to village they would bring the haberdashery, the leather goods, the imported glassware, pickled foods, wines or lamp oil. Anything which would not grow or could not be produced locally had to be traded, or perhaps manufactured by a specialist who travelled about the land selling his wares or services on a regular track. In remote places such itinerant tinkers, scissor sharpeners, roving cobblers or brush salesmen still turn up, in their season. Most of us, however, take our trade to settled shops, where all manner of wonderful things from the whole world are displayed for our consumption or admiration and use.

Fêtes and Fairs

In simpler times the Hiring Fair, or Horn Fair, or Horse or Goose Fair was a time to look forward to, when strangers brought together the whole population, to exchange goods, or livestock, or services or commodities and handcrafted wares. It was a chance for workers, dressed in the garb of their profession (the farm workers in smocks embroidered with the shepherd's crook, the dairymaid's stool or the ploughboy's horseshoe, all advertising their skills) to meet prospective employers. Standing in clusters with their horse-driving whips, or miniature sheaves of corn, their white aprons or moleskin waistcoats, they were ready for inspection by bosses who might require a carter, arable worker, a miller or head horse-man, as their traditional attire showed. Today many of these carefully made and long preserved garments are to be seen in folk museums, mutely telling of the work which used to need to be performed by an expert.

Today these local fairs tend to be mainly charity events, designed to raise money to restore the church roof, or help local children go on holidays. There are always a number of stalls which hark back to earlier times. Those selling fresh pastries and gateaux, which always go 'like hot cakes'; the plant stall, whose wares came from local gardens proving that anyone can grow tarragon or blue hydrangeas if they try; the book stall; the nearly new stall; the White Elephant stall, and these days, the computer program recycling stall; all ply for trade!

As well as the places where you can buy a

variety of commodities, there are always several rustic games of skill, such as 'bowling for a pig', the pig these days probably organically reared, slain, and divided up into neat packages for the freezer, rather than on the trotter, so to speak. There may well be a Tombola stall, where at the drawing of a correctly numbered ticket you might win a bottle of ketchup, a magnum of champagne or a voucher for a dinner for two at the local hostelry. You and your children can throw rings over bottles to win furry toys, or throw darts into targets for boxes of sweets. There might be a traditional coconut shy, or a stall where you can hurl hard balls at old china, as a way of releasing the tension brought on by missing all the coconuts; or perhaps wet sponges at one of your neighbours who is dressed up as the original Aunt Sally.

These days, where such fêtes are held in semi-urban places you may well get an influx of the local ethnic culture, perhaps expressed in music and dance, but more often as food. Greek kebabs, Jamaican patties, American hamburgers, Mexican enchiladas, Breton crêpes, Indonesian satay, and delicious vegetarian specialities from all over the place, usually, as fate would have it, set up next to the 'Real Flesh Company' offering organic venison sausages, and lamb and mint burgers! Food was always a part of the fair, from the old-fashioned hot pies, both sweet and savoury, to the roasts of whole beasts. An ox takes about eight hours to cook over hot charcoal, so a cook once told me, but a ram or sheep or decent-sized pig cooks well in the open air in an afternoon, and the scent wafting across the showground will attract custom from far and wide, as well as a small delegation of local vegans who will come and complain! Children, too, are often upset at seeing an entire carcase slowly sizzling in its own juices, over the glowing charcoal.

These roasts were nearly always an integral part of the celebration of a seasonal gathering, often called a 'Harvest Feast' or 'Reaping Supper' because it was a small reward to those in the locality, often not directly involved in the farming community, who had turned out to help get the hay or corn in. There would be gallons of the local ale, beer or cider, and nowadays, in this respect, homemade wines or fruit liqueurs are

making their presence felt. Eating was often followed by singing and dancing, and there may well have been various rituals concerned with the carting to the stackyard of the last load of hay. The horses, in the old days, would be beribboned and polished, and the hay, before the days of bales, had designs worked in it, or wild flowers scattered about or garlanding the wains. Here was the treasure of the land, garnered and displayed for all to see. It was the promise of survival through the winter for the livestock, and well-built hay ricks were a proud indication of a farmer's success. Children would ride the last load home, and be thrown to the top of the stack to help press down the aromatic hay, full of drying flowers and sweet clover.

Spells and Remedies

In a bad year, when the weather was wet or had been cold, and the grass was not long enough to make good hay, or what was cut mouldered in the fields, spells were cast and blame was attributed to fairies or bewitchment by envious neighbours. All kinds of charms were prevalent, to stop the milk turning sour, or to make the butter set:

> Come butter come, come butter come,
> St Peter stands at Heav'n's gate,
> Waiting for a buttered cake,
> So come butter come!

Natural flints with holes right through, called Holy Stones, were brought from the fields or beaches and hung with red ribbon or wool over the doors of cattle byres or horse stables to prevent any harm sickening the beasts, or milking the cows dry. Rowan wood was used as whip shafts by carters and drovers and the pleasant trees were often planted outside house doors to keep evil spirits at bay. Southernwood, an aromatic herb with woody stems, was laid among clothing to deter moths, and bunches of tansy and wormwood were hung up to keep flies out of the house.

Many herbal and traditional remedies were also sold at the July fairs, for it was a time of preserving by drying many of the most useful culinary plants – those used as ordinary medicine for the household and animals alike. Comfrey and boneset were used in cases of sprains or fractures; they were bound green about the injured place to form a dry and fairly solid splint, while the crushed plant helped reduce pain and swelling. Marsh woundwort was used for cuts got in the hay field when the careless scythe sliced into leg or foot, and the hardworked hands of the harvesters were anointed with a mixture of marigold petals and goosegrease. There are dozens of medicinal plants, many growing wild along old hedgerows or the edges of drainage ditches or streams, from which curative materials are extracted; and with the renewal of interest in all things natural and time-honoured, many products found in shops are derived from traditional, and sometimes extremely ancient, recipes. However, the use of live frogs to cure 'Thrush' in a child's throat, or live mice to cure whooping cough, doesn't seem to feature in orthodox treatment!

Independence Day, USA

In America, the Fourth of July, Independence Day, calls for major celebrations. The descendents of the early settlers thought of America as their home, while still regarding England as the mother country. But the English government maintained that as colonial subjects they must still pay taxes to England. They resented having to pay this, when they got nothing for it and had no Members of Parliament in London to speak for them. Their slogan was 'No taxation without representation'.

Another issue was the charging of duty on imports of tea. In 1773 some colonists dressed up as native Americans and threw about 300 chests of tea overboard from a ship in Boston harbour as a protest. This action was called the 'Boston Tea Party'.

Eventually in 1775 war broke out against the English forces controlling the colony. This went on for eight years; finally the colonists won and were recognised as an independent self-governing nation. On 4 July 1776 the colonists had issued their Declaration of Independence. The famous Liberty Bell, on which is inscribed 'Proclaim liberty throughout the land, unto all the inhabitants thereof' was rung to celebrate the adoption of the Declaration, and is still rung every Fourth of July. All across the United States it is celebrated as a public holiday with historical pageants and parades, with firework displays and barbecues in the evening. Many people celebrate by trips to the countryside or to the beach.

July Festivals

July, in common with the other summer months, is also the time of the Flower Shows, the Beer and Wine Making exhibitions, the local Fuchsia Growers summer display and the wonderful Flower Festivals in village churches. It is a time for bell ringing, both the elevating peals rung from the steeples, and the chimes of handbell ringing, which today is a musical and sophisticated art form. From simple chimes these ringers now offer classical music, songs from popular theatrical productions and more modern renditions of familiar tunes, rung out note by note. Fruits and vegetables, flowers and shrubs become works of art in sunlit marquees on the village green, and displays of sheep-dog handling, folk dances, parades of old fashioned vehicles, marching bands and fancy dress all add music, fun and competition to these cheerful occasions. Steam organs, bagpipers, fifes and drums, singers, folk musicians, hurdygurdy players and steel bands bring along their own dimensions of sounds.

The other modern addition to the Show circuit is that of the Fun Fair, Victorian in essence, with its originally steam-driven roundabouts with their galloping horses and other animals, Chair-o-planes, Bumper Cars, and Ferris Wheels, whose twinkling lights circle aloft in the summer nights. Now such rides feature space ships, or antigravitational Walls of Death, or scary Ghost Trains. With these commercial enterprises, moving from fairground to fairground throughout the season go the Shooting Galleries, the Hoop-las, the Roll-a-Ball games, with their glittering prizes, and onion-scented takeaway food stands. Again, although hi-tech has computerised the controls of the whirling cars, or electrified the

Well Dressing

In July one of the old customs which combines a religious work with a kind of flower show is the art of Well Dressing. At different times of year, all over the country, both traditionally and in revival, the village well or source of water is dressed. Usually this dressing takes the form of making pictures which illustrate Biblical scenes on beds of damp clay, with flowers, petals, leaves, mosses and coloured plant materials. These mosaic pictures are fitted into a frame around the stone facade of the well house or spout. Sometimes these events record a local blessing when, for example, the well did not dry up during a severe drought, or when a new spring was found at a time of need. Some such wells are dedicated to Christian saints, often female, who took over from the older, pagan spirits who guarded the waters, or the sacred women, noted in the Arthurian legends, who were keepers of fountains, often associated with healing. It was the rape and desecration of these holy ladies which partly led to the barrenness of the Wasteland, and the Quest for the Holy Grail which would free and cleanse the waters.

Throughout many counties, from Gloucestershire to Yorkshire and from Cornwall to Derbyshire, where there are situated very famous wells, there are well-dressing ceremonies at the end of July. In Buxton, at St Anne's well, a spring previously dedicated to the pagan Goddess, Arnemetia, ceremonies have taken place since Roman times. Pins were offered at Bradwell, before Easter, to ensure a good supply of water throughout the year, and this well is dressed in

pretty patterns of flashing lights, the original ideas are far older.

At feasts and festivals there used to be all manner of sports, games and competitions, especially in the bare hayfields, or when a local ruler died, according to the Celtic Chroniclers in Dark Age Britain. Horse races, archery contests, games of wit or dexterity, races where the competitors had to leap as high as their shoulder, and run under obstacles as low as their knees, were popular events. Today we make our dogs perform these feats! There were throwing competitions, originally of tree trunks, as in the Scottish sport of Tossing the Caber, or hurling boulders; now sometimes they still require contestants to throw a bale of hay over a high cord with a pitchfork, or toss a wellington boot further, higher or more accurately than the others. Some aspects change, yet the underlying traditions continue in a new guise. Do look anew when you hear the jingle of Morris bells, the clatter of racing hooves, the thud of falling bodies at your local fête or Fair, for there you will find re-enactments of some very ancient sports or competitions. If you participate, even to a very minor degree, you too will share the on-going blessing or satisfaction of at least having been there, taken part or won your useless prize. You will have gained vicarious benefits from your efforts or by the act of joining in.

early August. Sometimes the ceremony was founded of the relief from Plague in the fourteenth century, or some special piece of luck which benefited the community served by that water source. Today there is usually a service of dedication for the assembled picture when the local vicar says his piece, and maybe the section of the Bible whose story is retold in flowers is read. There may be a procession, brass band music or prayer, depending on the feelings of those involved. Although these works of art are quite ephemeral, the effects realised with natural substances has to be seen to be appreciated in its effect and delicacy.

St Swithin's Day

Another watery feast in July is that of St Swithin, by all accounts a humble man who, as Bishop of Winchester, in Hampshire, in the Saxon period, requested that after his death he be laid among the ordinary folk in the churchyard, where the rain might fall on his resting place and the footsteps of passersby tread over him. This was duly done and many miracles were recorded as a result of the sick and troubled visiting his common grave. But then the worthy monks of Winchester decided that it was not right that the late Bishop should lie in such humble soil and moved his resting place to an elaborate shrine inside the cathedral. Somehow the saint made his displeasure at this removal quite plain and declared that it would rain for forty days and forty nights, which in the middle of summer was not appreciated, so after a considerable downpour the saint's remains were returned to their outdoor setting. Today it is said that if it rains on St Swithin's day, 15 July, it will continue to do so for forty days, but if that day stays dry, so will the next forty days. If it does rain about that date it is considered lucky for the fruit growers, for such water swells the developing apples and pears, though even they probably prefer short showers rather than continual rain.

Rushbearing

Rushbearing is another old church celebration, more popular in the midlands and north than the south, when new rushes were strewn on the floors of churches and houses, before carpets were in common use. In some places this festival is a bit later in the year, when huge carts are filled with freshly-cut water rushes, and processions wind through the villages. The haycock-shaped pile of rushes was decked with flowered ropes, branches of green leaves and had mottoes or blessings worked into banners on its sides. In Cumbria, a band of small girls dressed in green carry a sheet of rushes, and others create 'bearings', which are elaborate decorations made out of these stiff green spikes, in the shape of

crosses, crowns or harps. Between the end of June and the middle of August many such activities fill the air of the Lake District with the sharp, peppery scent of crushed rushes as they are shaped into decorative forms for bearing to the local centrepiece.

'Green grow the rushes O', a many-versed song, may well have come from such a ceremony, although I haven't heard it sung at one:

I'll sing you One O, Green grow the rushes O,
What is your One O? Green Grow the rushes O.
One is One and all alone, ever more to be so!

Two are the Lily White Boys, perhaps early Morris Men, 'clothed all in green, ho ho.' Three are the Rivals; Four are the Gospel Makers; Five are the Symbols at your door, perhaps the magical protective pentagram, the five-pointed star. Six are the Six Proud Walkers; Seven are the Seven Stars in the sky, probably a reference to the Plough; Eight are the April Rainers, and so on. There are several alternative versions, and both Christians and pagans have found sense in variations of the general theme, to do with symbols and the magical power of numbers.

Another simple summer time pursuit, this time concerned with water, was the tying of strips of rag or ribbon to trees as offerings for a healing, particularly in cases of eye disease. Pilgrimages for this purpose were often made by sufferers who sought out a lucky number, either three or five, of different wells or springs with healing properties. They would bathe their sores in each and ask a blessing, leaving in return a streamer of cloth in a nearby tree to fret away the disease in the wind.

Wild Flowers

July is a month of pink in the hedgerows and untended parts of garden; and in any open space where fire has passed, the tall spears of dark green-leaved rose bay willowherb cluster in mauve-pink splendour. The striped pink and white bells of the field bindweed train over fences and in unconquered corners of the rose bed. The purple thistles on their crisp and spikey stems hum regally with black and yellow bumblebees,

each furred and velveted with dusted pollen. Gold, too, is visible, in the centres of the peppery white daisies of feverfew, a herb recently rediscovered for its alleviation of migraine, and long used to calm the fevered brow of anyone suffering hot summer nights. The most convenient form is that of its relative, chamomile, used dried in tea. Corn marigolds and all the unpalatable dark green plants of ragwort are found in some of the less sprayed, cultivated lands showing the lack of the farmer's personal attention with a reaping hook.

In some of the July flower shows there are opportunities for children to gather wild flowers and make small posies, arrangements of blooms and leaves in an old shoe, or ones only a few inches high, or of a particular colour. July offers an entire rainbow of all the natural hues, from the flame scarlet of corn poppies across to the brilliant blue of wild chicory. Yellow is always there with buttercups running like sheets of gold across the open meadows, studded here and there with the taller white of dog daisies, the pinks of all the vetch tribe, the mauves of mallows in the damper spots, and the magenta clusters of everlasting pea, sadly without its cultivated sweet pea sister's perfume and grace.

Wild roses throng the hedges, and the green flowered black bryony, later to yield poisonous yet fascinating strings of green turning to red berries, trails among the greenery. Binding together other shrub branches in their scramble to the light are still sweet scented honeysuckle and wild clematis, 'Grandfather's Beard', which later will shroud the bare branches with its white tufts. This is a rich but forgotten heritage, the hundreds of varieties of wild flowers and trees and their decorative seeds which we can so usefully employ in our seasonal decorations.

Bawming the Thorn

In Appleton in Cheshire there is a tree-decorating ceremony, called 'Bawming the Thorn', or adorning the hawthorn tree which is said to be an offspring of the famous Glastonbury Thorn. The honoured tree is actually not very old and currently surrounded by iron railings. Children dressed in garlands of flowers, carrying posies and other beribboned or floral tributes, come and deck out the thorn tree with ribbons and flowers. This is a modern survival of the old idea of dressing up a tree as a symbol of life, or of healing or luck-bringing power. The pre-Christians in Britain did not make effigies of their sacred deities, but held holy things made by Creation, such as special trees, unusual rocks, springs or wells. Each had an additional spirit or Maiden, who might be consulted as a kind of local oracle, or as a healer, or problem solver.

Swan Upping

Another waterborne happening in July is the tradition of 'Swan Upping', which is the essence of the Swan Voyage made by rowing boats on part of the urban Thames. Swans are Royal birds, and most of them belong to the Crown, but the Companies or Guilds of Vintners and Dyers have

had rights to own, capture and, in earlier times, eat swans taken from the river. Because cygnets are still with their parents in July, it is then that a small fleet of the Queen's Swanherd, and representatives of the Guild of Vintners, in a livery of green, and Dyers in blue, capture and 'up' any swans they discover. The Pen and Cob's beaks are examined to see who owns them, for all birds belonging to the Livery Companies are marked, with one nick cut for the Dyers, and two for the

Vintners. If the birds are unmarked they are Royal. All are then set free. In the case of mixed marriages, the cygnets are shared between the two parties, some being marked to indicate each side of their parentage. The various Swanherds have a care for the birds during the rest of the year.

Many swans have died as a result of pollution of the Thames, or because they have eaten lead shot from fishing weights which has lodged in the mud at the bottom of the river where they feed. Although the use of lead shot for fishing weights has been banned as a result of these poisonings, some of it, lost by generations of fishermen, still lies in the riverbanks, along with discarded hooks and lines which injure or trap all kinds of waterfowl each year. The tradition of marking swans is recorded in the name of pubs called the 'Swan with two Necks' or nicks, meaning a Vintner's house.

Sirius, the Dog Star

In July the 'Dog Days' fall. They take their name from the Dog Star, Sirius, which is visible in Britain from the first week in the month. This star's heliacal rising, when it appears red on the horizon and turns greenish blue at its zenith, was supposed to herald a time of dearth, with droughts, searing heat and unpleasant winds, which made work in the fields particularly tiring. People suffered all kinds of ills then, and were advised against the remedy, applied at other times, of letting blood, either of people or animals. Any disease which struck during the time from the rising of Sirius through to its departure about 12 August was likely to be more lasting and unpleasant than one caught at other times.

In other places, however, the sight of Sirius on the horizon was a sign of hope. This was especially true in ancient Egypt, where this brilliant star's appearance marked the rising and flooding of the silt-rich, fertile waters of the Nile. Again there is a 'dog' connection, for among the varied tribes of Egyptian deities, Anubis, the Guide through this world and the next, has the head of a jackal, or small hound. His appearance was a sign that new life would return to the dried-up banks of the great river, and the black, rich, alluvial soil washed down from the mountains would restore greenness and allow agriculture to continue. The ancient name for Egypt was 'Khem', the black land, and from this was derived the name of the Black Art, Alchemy.

Sacred Sites and Mizmazes

July is of course a great time for visiting outdoor historic sites, or museums and places of interest. The solar head shown above is that which was found on the facade of the vast Roman Temple to the Goddess Sulis at Bath. The huge, bearded head represents her champion and protector, and may be a depiction of Bran, the Celtic Sun God. It has a number of interesting symbols around it, uncommon in Roman religious art, and seldom found among the Celts, who, on the whole, did not make images of their gods. In his beard and round his neck are some snakes, which form the Torc, or gold necklace worn by kings and nobles. Snakes are also depicted, in pre-Christian settings, as symbols of healing and wisdom, both of which are attributes of Sulis herself. The figure has large ears with which to listen to the prayers of supplicants, he also has wings with which to fly to their aid, and the locks of hair above his head seem to be flames or the rays of the sun. In this way he represents the Elements, earth or watery snake/serpents, airy wings, and fire flames. His calm, almost hypnotic gaze peers out from the rebuilt face in the Roman Museum at Bath; it must have been a very powerful thing to

encounter in the first century or so of the Christian era.

His face may be studied free of charge and at closer quarters in the maze which was built in the late 1980s, close to the river below Pulteney Bridge, where it forms the centre piece of an elliptical labyrinth in the gardens there. Around his face are other aspects of the legends; Apollo, the Roman Sun God with his lyre, the sacred pigs of King Bladud, whose legend tells how he was healed by following the wallowing swine into the hot marshes around the thermal spring, in times gone by. There is a beautiful Pegasus, and other Gods and Goddesses whose power has been felt and worshipped in this sacred city, in its basin of seven hills.

Mizmazes used to be cut out of the turf and walked as a kind of meditation. Around the country several public ones survive, and it is the kind of thing which owners of stately homes are constructing to interest visitors. Not all mazes are like the Hampton Court Maze, with its high hedges and confusing pathways. Some are the older, one-way, semi-circling labyrinths, with only one path wound back upon itself. These are carved on rocks near Tintagel, in Cornwall, and marked on various beaches from Sweden to America, with stones outlining the walls. They are seen on ancient coins and Greek pots. There is even a reference in Shakespeare's Midsummer Night's Dream, when Titania complains that these ancient, magical patterns are falling into decay: 'The Nine Men's Morris is fill'd up with mud, and the Quaint mazes on the wanton green, for want of tread, are indistinguishable ...'. There used to be lots of them, called Troy Towns, or Shepherd's Races, or they appear on maps as 'mizmazes' though few on common land can be walked. As a mental or meditational exercise they have very strange effects. There is a huge labyrinthine path up Glastonbury Tor, redis-covered a few years ago by Geoffrey Ashe, the Arthurian scholar, who now lives there.

July, then, is full of summer activity, of special places to visit and community events to attend. Whether you are going to a Summer Fête or a traditional fair, or sharing the songs and music of a Music Festival, like those at Bath or Cheltenham or Edinburgh, where thousands of performers, classical, fringe and beyond the fringe, appear in concert halls, fields, on a village green or in a city shopping precinct, the desire to join with others in some kind of shared gathering is terrific. Some of these summer occasions are one-day events, others last weeks; some are centred round a tiny community, or single craftworker, others have casts of thousands; yet all, in their individual ways, recall the atmosphere and jollity, the exchanges of goods and opinions, the interaction of musicians and dancers and audience of similar occasions that entertained and benefited our ancestors.

CANCER, THE CRAB

Most of July is ruled by the water sign, Cancer, the Crab, whose planet is the changeable moon. Those born between about 21 June to 22 July share some of the characteristics of this hard-shelled but soft-hearted creature. Liking to be on the fringes of several worlds, just as crabs wander between the seas or rivers and the shoreline, Cancer folk often seem to bridge several places or activities. Their habit of scuttling sideways shows their diplomacy and tact, for they feel hurts very strongly and can withdraw into their shells in defence. They may be loyal friends, hanging on through difficult times, when less tenacious colleagues drop away. They are dreamy and romantic individuals, and are sometimes slow to make decisions, but they are shrewd and perceptive, often being quite psychic, a tendency shared by all the water signs. They have good memories and make good business partners, caring mothers, and wise counsellors, although, because they can be quite touchy, those who share their lives need to learn to be tactful in order not to upset them. They can be extremely perceptive and intuitive, coming up with unusual solutions to problems. Cancer folk include the Elizabethan mathematician and astrologer, Dr John Dee, who advised Queen Elizabeth I, and also Dr Margaret Murray, an archaeologist who did great works in Egypt. Some, like John D. Rockefeller and John Jacob Astor, became extremely rich. Princess Diana is another Cancer person who has made a place for herself in the public domaine. Helen Keller, blind authoress, and Mary Baker Eddy who founded the Christian Science philosophy, are Cancerians best known for their good works.

These summer born folk are often people with rich inner lives, with thoughts and ambitions not shared even with their family and friends. As children they are always being told to concentrate, or watch what they are doing because they would prefer to be off in their own interior dream-worlds, or lost in the pages of a book. In later-life these interior thoughts can lead to great creativity, artistic works and even inspired pronouncements. They may become 'channelers' or succeed as guides and spiritual counsellors, but mainly outside the orthodox religious path. The new fields of psychology or even parapsychology may appeal to them where they can demonstrate their insight into the conditions of others, or give free rein to their psychic impressions.

The colours and jewels which are most attractive to the Cancer person include emerald, both as a colour and as a gem, and silver which is the metal associated with the moon. Moonstones, crystal, pearls, coral, cats' eyes and aquamarines, especially if set in silver or silvery mounts, please them. They look well in white, but may prefer other water colours, muted blues and sea greens, as well as soft pastel shades rather than brilliant ones.

Rabbit with Mushrooms

1 medium-sized fresh rabbit
2 oz/60g/¼ cup butter
2 oz/60g/½ cup plain flour
1 lb/500g/4 cups sliced mushrooms
1 lb/500g/3 cups small white onions
1 clove garlic (crushed or chopped)
¾ pint/45cl/2 cups white wine
salt and pepper
1 tbsp chopped parsley

Cut the rabbit into about six pieces. Melt the butter in a casserole and brown the rabbit pieces in it. Thicken the fat with the flour when the meat is browned. Add the mushrooms, onions, garlic, white wine and salt and pepper, and cook in a 325°C/170°F/Mark 3 oven for about 2 hours, until the rabbit meat is tender.

Serve the rabbit sprinkled with the chopped parsley.

Summer Pudding

July may well bring a glut of the type of soft fruit which is not always nice raw in a fruit salad. The answer is to use it to make excellent, traditional Summer Puddings.

about 1 lb/500g/4 cups mixed berries
  (raspberries, strawberries, red and black
  currants, even cherries and loganberries if
  available)
six to eight slices stale white or stale fine
  brown bread, crusts removed
sugar to taste
packet raspberry, strawberry or cherry jelly
  (optional)
¼ pint/15cl/⅔ cup boiling water (optional)

Simmer the berries in the minimum amount of water – just enough to soften the fruit without boiling it to a pulp. Meanwhile, line a pudding basin with the bread slices, reserving a couple for the top. Sweeten the fruit with a little sugar or, if preferred, dissolve the jelly in the water and mix this into the fruit.

Spoon the fruit into the bread-lined basin. Place a lid of bread slices on the top and a saucer which fits into the basin on top of that, then add a suitable weight to press it down. The pudding should be left to get cold or, if mixed with jelly, set. When you are ready to serve the pudding, turn it out to form a small red mountain. It is delicious accompanied by clotted cream.

Rose Petal Wine

If there is an abundance of roses growing in your garden, this is a good use for them.

6 pints/3.5 litres/7 US pints scented rose
  petals (no insects!)
8 pints/5 litres/10 US pints water
3 lb/1.5kg/6 cups sugar
2 lemons, zest peeled, juice squeezed
2 tsp wine yeast, dissolved in a little warm
  water

Tip the rose petals into a large bowl. Bring the water to the boil, add the sugar and dissolve it; add the lemon zest, boil together briefly, then allow to cool. Pour the water over the rose petals, then add the lemon juice and the activated wine yeast.

Cover the wine, then leave it to ferment for seven days, stirring it daily. At the end of this time, strain it into a fermentation jar with an airlock and allow it to ferment to a finish. Bottle the wine and allow it to age, so that the scent of roses develops – its colour will depend on the roses' colour.

Rose petals (with their bitter white 'heel' removed) can also be used to decorate summer salads. Other flowers, such as borage, violets, nasturtiums, marjoram, and marigold petals also make a colourful addition to salads.

MAKE A FANCY DRESS
WAISTCOAT

This is another use for the dozens of plastic carrier bags which the average household seems to accumulate, including the pretty ones with holes in which no longer serve their carrying purpose. A simple sleeveless jacket can be part of a fancy dress competition, or a fashion show or charity event.

Find a bag wide enough to fit the individual across the shoulders and then cut out armholes, a front opening and neck line as in Fig 2. You may need to trim off handles. Decorate with fringes cut from contrasting coloured strips (Fig 3) and stuck on with sticky tape, stapled or sewn on (start from the bottom and work up). Appliqué flowers or animals, for example, can also be attached. The back can be a grand design in multi-colours, cut-out leaves or feathers or pretty patterns.

The finished jacket will stand up to a bit of rain, and matching hats, skirts or shorts can be invented by those good at sewing and design. Fastenings can be with ties or loops and buttons where necessary.

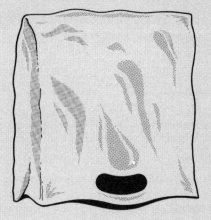

Fig. 1.

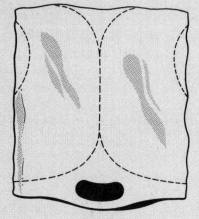

Fig. 2.

Fig. 3.

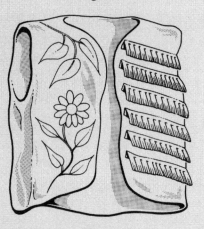

Fig. 4.

AUGUST

There came three men from out of the West, Their victory for to try,
As they had sworn a solemn oath, John Barleycorn must die ....
But soon came men with their sharp scythes, And chopped him to the knee,
They rolled him and tied him by the waist, and served him barb'rously ...

from *'John Barleycorn'*, traditional song

August was always the month of harvesting, first the barley and oats, then the wheat. The workers were in the cornfields from first light until nightfall when the weather was dry, cutting, stooking, carrying, and making the cornricks. Now, as soon as the percentage of water in the grain falls sufficiently the combine harvesters are brought in, and the corn is cut and threshed out of the straw in one noisy, diesel-fumed operation by huge, florid machines, which cost as much as a house! Where is the singing over that racket, the communal effort, the slaving in the baking fields with only a cup of warm cider and a lump of bread and cheese to sustain a fifteen-hour day? Neither method has the rural charm that eighteenth century pictures of reapers in the field evoke, the leisured cutting with rhythmically swinging sickles to rustic tunes under a warm sky, with maids in low cut gowns nurturing the heated workers with sweet pastries and cool ale. However the corn is cut, European grain mountains notwithstanding, it is hard work, and as the culmination of many a farmer's year, a time of anxiety and concern.

Crop Circles

These days the golden fields are enriched by mysterious 'Crop Circles' and flattened patterns in the standing crops. These are proving a new and lucrative harvest for some people. All kinds of explanations, from freak weather conditions, mating and playful animals, helicopters and mysterious forces from under the Earth or out of the sky have been suggested. Certainly reckless young farmers may account for the appearance of some of these increasingly strange designs, but in general their symmetry, and the way in which something in the chemical structure of the crops has been affected, cannot be explained. They are seen primarily in the South of England, but a variety of similar strange formations have been seen in Japan, America and Australia, where the open land presents a similar surface.

Although it was in the 1980s that these strange happenings became more widely publicised, reports of areas of mysteriously flattened plants were recorded back as far as the 1940s with rare sightings possibly going back many hundreds of years. Tests on the actual stems of the wheat seem to indicate that though they are bent over, and laid flat on the ground in neat vortices, they are still growing, but that some sort of change has been made to the structure at the point of the bend. At present no one has seen a circle being formed, except the fake ones, obviously, when those involved must have seen their handiwork. There have been reports of orange lights in the sky, and technicians investigating the phenomenon have measured strange readings on their equipment, or heard and recorded unusual noises.

There are many places where such events have been seen, but one of the factors which links these areas is that many of them have ancient earthworks, tracks or mounds and barrows near them. Quite a few of the fields near Silbury Hill and the Avebury complex have had elaborate patterns made in them in the latter part of the 1980s, and one theory about these circles is that they are forming over ancient ritual sites. Some of these might have been the footings of circular dwelling huts, or dancing grounds, or stockades, perhaps made with thorn bushes rather than with posts knocked into the ground, as used to be common, but as yet no archaeological investigations have confirmed this possible link. There may indeed be some mysterious energy, which is sufficient to bend over growing crops, manifesting from places which were once sacred, as open air Temples to the Sky Gods, or gathering places of the tribes. At present we don't know, but it is clear that the patterns revealed are getting more complicated, and so even more mysterious.

Harvest Time Traditions

To the Anglo-Saxons the start of August was known as *Hlafmas* or Loaf-mass or, in Scotland, 'Lughnasad', the Feast of the Celtic Sun God, Lugh, who was seen as a God of Light whose spirit was the life of the growing corn. The Lammas feast was both a celebration and a kind of remembrance of this energy which was changed from a living force in the corn to a static one in the cut sheaves. In Britain, during August, there used to be a public holiday called 'Wakes Week' during which as many people as possible were brought from their ordinary occupations to help with the harvesting. Today, mechanisation has taken care of much of the work but the holiday has survived as Bank Holiday Monday at the end of the month.

In the old days everyone was expected to help with the cutting, binding into sheaves, stooking or carting, or by providing food and drink for the workers, or perhaps joining in the rabbit hunts by surrounding the area of uncut corn and catching as many of these animals as possible as they were driven out of the standing grain, on which they had no doubt been feeding. Rabbit Pie and Stew was a valuable addition to the table of the hard-working reapers, and there are lots of old recipes involving cooking rabbits with cider or beer. This was not really a form of ritual sacrifice but a way of getting rid of a pest. Sadly, today, many of the great combine harvesters wipe out fieldmice in their intricate nests woven in among the corn stalks, as well as rabbits, birds and all kinds of wild creatures too slow, or too confused by these great grinding machines, to escape.

There is a tradition, which still survives as a local custom in parts of Cornwall, called the ceremony of 'Crying the Neck', which is a kind of sacrificial act, not performed on any animal, but on the corn itself. Traditionally it was supposed to be unlucky to cut the last sheaf of wheat, or to be the last farmer in the area to complete the harvesting, so a kind of game was developed whereby all the harvesters would gather round the last upright tuft of corn, and standing back, take their small sickles and hurl them at the base of the corn, so no one knew for certain who had cut down the last stem, and so symbolically slain the Corn Spirit. From this last sheaf the best ears of corn would be taken and woven into a Corn Dolly. This would be placed in a special display, often over the hearth, which in British homes acts as a kind of altar, decked with pictures of the family and loved ones, or favourite ornaments, candlesticks and the like. Here it should stay, being admired all the winter, until the spring sowing, when the corn would be shaken out of the ears and added to the rest of the seed corn before sowing, as this ensured that the magical fertility saved from the last strands of the previous harvest was shared among the new crop.

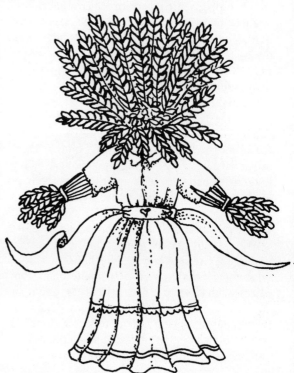

The 'Crying the Neck' ceremony is blessed by church men in some Cornish parishes, but prayers and charms are still spoken in Cornish. There is a cry of *"Yma genef! Yma genef!"* answered by *"Pandr'us genes? Pandr'us genes?"* again answered with *"Pen Yar! Pen Yar!"* This means roughly "I have got it!" requiring the question, "What have you got?" to which the answer is *"Pen Yar"* – literally a hen's head, rather than a 'neck' of corn. Maybe this was some kind of bird offering; after all, the Glorious Twelfth, when shooting game birds begins, is only days away. There may be another sacred act here, though, for many of the forms of Corn Dolly that are woven are in the form of the Earth Mother, the Corn Queen, or the feminine Horn of Plenty. It is she who is fertile, it is her body, the Earth, which brings forth the grain in due season, or she whose fertility that fails. Just as eggs appear as gifts of the Sacred Hare at the Spring or Sowing Festival, may not the one who laid those magical eggs be considered here as the Hen who is cut down so that her bounty may be shared by the people along with their new flour?

The other colour especially associated with harvest is red. Many of the different local variations of the Corn Dolly are tied with scarlet ribbons. The horses once used on farms nearly always had their manes plaited and bound up with red ribbons, and sometimes garlands of field poppies and the blue corn flowers were hung about the harvest, or set into the loads of sheaves as they were carted from the fields to the barns or stackyards. In magic, red has always been associated with the Life Force itself, because blood is red. Red flowers are incorporated into bouquets presented to some of the ladies who have a ceremonial part to play in these seasonable gatherings. The representative of the Earth Mother, as Lady of the Feast, as Maiden, or Harvest Queen, is offered floral tributes in which the life-blood colour usually features. Red is fire, energy, the heat of the Sun, and the few flowers in England which are naturally bright red (the poppies and that poor man's weathervane, the scarlet pimpernel being the most common) are always thought special.

This season was, by everyone's consideration, the most critical in the entire year. To a certain extent it still is, although modern growing methods tend to end up with a surplus of grain in the world in the North, which is set aside and saved for years of hardship, to trade with other nations less well endowed, or exchange through world food markets for other commodities. The all-important factor over which the farmers and growers have no control is the weather. It could have been an excellent growing season with ripening grain and other foodstuffs in every field, yet a heavy rainstorm or hail stones can flatten, soak and ruin any crop, making it impossible to harvest, or rain can make the fields so wet that no heavy machinery can even go upon them for fear of sinking in. High winds from uncommon directions can lay corn flat, or affect parts of fields so that they will not stand and ripen evenly, which is a far more critical problem with the use of combine harvesters than it was in the old days. A combine must have dry grain which can be knocked out of the husks within the machine, whereas when corn was stooked until dry, as each area was ready it could be carted for threshing by steam driven machinery.

Some of the changes in the weather in recent years, brought on by pollution and thinning of the ozone layer, are leading to more periods of drought, the raised possibility of hurricane force winds, which naturally occur about once in seventy-five years, and greater heat or longer periods of dryness. None of these will help our kinds of plants and trees, nurtured in the traditional sorts of wind or weather. We may have to start growing olives and expanding our vineyards, and exchange our corn harvest for gathering maize. Instead of specially brewed harvest ales we would have to try a sort of Octoberfest which they have in Germany, in September, to dance and sing as the grapes are picked. These things may come, if the strange weather we have had for the last few years persists.

Walking Week

One of the older traditions around mid-August was not only Wakes Week, but Walking Week, when those employed in factories and mills took time off to walk in the countryside, or enjoy sea air, long before package trips to the Costa Brava were dreamed of, or the ubiquitous flight to the sun after an entertaining few hours or days at the local airport! Some of these Walks had a religious facet, in that they were a kind of small pilgrimage. Some held earlier in the year, around Whitsun, were called 'Walking Days' when rival churches laid on attractions to draw in visitors. The ladies were expected to dress in white, and little girls to carry posies of flowers; there are still such processions through the streets of some Lancashire towns. They are drawn from Sunday Schools and local church Clubs who follow their embroidered banners along traditional routes, lined with onlookers. There is often a local brass or silver band to serenade the Walk. This may recall many different processions in celebration of local events or good luck, many going well back into history, but many wiped out by the austerity of the Reformation which tried, and largely succeeded, in separating the church from joy, music, celebration, ancient and probably pagan customs, or dancing in the churchyard, which the congregation must have enjoyed.

It was this same regime which cut down the May Poles, got rid of sacred trees, dismissed

well-dressing as idolatry, and filled in the mazes and some of the great hill figures because they were ancient symbols of life and love. They discouraged even the singing of hymns, which to many people was the only instrumental music they might hear, if there was no local band, or musicians. Before the seventeenth century there must have been thousands of village celebrations, ritual dances and walks to healing wells on special Saints' Days or in remembrance of lucky days. It was during the Reformation that the reverence for nature and the blessings of natural phenomena were wiped out. Trees, standing stones, springs or even large rivers were seen as being aspects of the Creator placed near communities to be of use, and so it was usual to make offerings of flowers, fruit, bread or beer at such places, so that the luck or blessing would continue. After the Reformation, it was thought that nature was there to be conquered, overcome and controlled; and we are now learning to our cost that this is not the case.

Royal National Eisteddfod

Another event which makes August a celebration, especially in Wales, is the Royal National Eisteddfod, which year by year, moves from North to South Wales and back, choosing a new site for its tented city each time. It has a long history, as a festival of Welsh Culture, with music, dance, poetry and song, as well as many other aspects of the spiritual life which our ancestors valued. Not only do they erect a huge pavilion but they build a new stone circle for the Gorsedd each year, where, at the beginning of the eight-day event, the Arch Druid asks peace upon the proceedings.

As well as many on-going competitions during the Eisteddfod for singing, dancing, playing various instruments and arts and crafts, the two main events are the Crowning of the Bard and the Chairing of the Bard. Each is a celebration of poetry, written in the Welsh language. (In fact the entire event is conducted in Welsh, with TV and radio commentaries on the most ceremonial parts in English, for the dreaded *sais* beyond the Principality.) It has been a custom since at least the fourteenth century to award a prize of a crown or chair to a leading poet. This Celtic custom was revived and embellished by 'Iolo Morgannwg', the poet, writer and translator from Welsh, Edward Williams, in the eighteenth century, when many things antiquarian or traditional were being rediscovered. It was he who described the kinds of robes the Druids wear, both of the Welsh Gorsedd, and those who are more spiritually minded, with white for the highest grade, blue for the bards, poets and musicians, and green for the Ovates, or teachers and historians. Members of all three orders are present at the main ceremonies, as well as robed members of the Cornish, Breton and Isle of Man's own Gorsedd circles, and visitors from the Gaelic speaking Irish and Scottish cultural associations are welcomed. Each usually speaks in his or her own ancient language and then offers greetings in Welsh.

The first prize of a silver crown is offered for the best cycle of poetry in Welsh to a set theme such as 'Sparks' or 'Veins' or 'Dust'; and competition is fierce, for being a Crowned or Chaired Bard is a great honour at a time when cultural activities receive less and less national support. The adjudicators will have deliberated for some weeks over the entries, all of which have to be submitted with a *nom de plume* so that local rivalries or family ties cannot affect the judging. In the dark pavilion, the silver trumpets call and answer as the brightly robed Gorsedd arrive in procession. After speeches of welcome, adjudication and comments, which last some time, the spotlight may dance over the packed crowd. Somewhere among the four thousand or so spectators is the man or woman whose work has been chosen, although in some years either the Crown or the Chair is not awarded if the judges think the standard not worthy. The Bardic name of the winner is called and in a hushed moment a small figure is picked out in light. The winner is dressed in purple, and led to the platform to receive the Crown. Made of silver and reflecting aspects of the life of the Town where the Eisteddfod is that year, it is a beautiful example of some local silversmith's art, and a very worthy prize.

The other award, of a Chair, which takes place on the Thursday of the week, is for *Cynghanedd*,

an archaic form of verse wherein not only is there a rhyming pattern at the ends of the lines, but certain vowel and consonantal sounds within the lines have to conform too. Poets may submit up to two hundred lines of this brain and language torturing verse! The Chair the poet wins is a real one made by a local craftsworker, but it used in earlier times to be a model in silver.

As with the Crown, if the Chair is being awarded, the recipient is told of his or her triumph beforehand but is sworn to secrecy. At the moment of presentation the winner is sought with a moving spotlight in the dark tent. Again, in ritual robes, the winner is led forwards to take a place beside the Arch Druid. The Sword bearer partially unsheathes the mighty ceremonial sword, calling for peace in all parts of the world, and is answered, *Heddwch!* by the assembled company. Welsh-speaking little girls, clad in green tunics and garlands of wild flowers, dance before him, gathering up posies from the ground as the inspired poet is supposed to garner words. They then arrange the flowers into a beautiful and emotional offering. The winner is offered the 'Hirlas' Horn of welcoming wine, though none seems to be provided, and a bouquet of flowers by another of the lovely ladies from the area. He appears to gain neither wine, nor flowers nor the ladies to take home now, but who knows what he used to be offered!

It is wonderful that words and poetry should be so highly rewarded in a time when it is military leaders or unlettered people who so often seem to matter most in a materialistic world. The honouring of poets, singers, dancers and musicians during this week-long festival celebrates all that is good and peaceful in life. All these arts had their roots in a sacred tradition, and these Bardic Orders, even if slightly over-dramatic, recall an ancient care given by those concerned with the Spiritual side of life as opposed to its mundane aspects, to all who sought learning, or art or music. The atmosphere is wonderful and unmatched by any other large event, and even if you know no Welsh, it is an occasion which gladdens the heart and restores the soul.

The Burry Man

From a mass performance to one of solo endurance, bring on the 'Burry Man', a fellow covered from head to foot with the hooked fruits of the burdock plant. During mid-August in South Queensferry, South Lothian, this strange and archaic character (supported by two helpers, and carrying in his necessarily outstretched arms poles with flowers at their tops) makes a long and uncomfortable pilgrimage. The costume is made of thick flannel and even covers his face, and the whole thing is completely covered with spikey burrs. A Scottish flag is wrapped around his waist, and once inside this armour-stiff and very heavy costume he has to continue all day, walking slowly round the burgh. He goes from house to house along a seven-mile track, and his two supporters, who have no costumes, collect money and gifts on his behalf. Brightly dressed children dance about him, and all except the Burry Man himself raise a great shout to bring out the householders and their gifts.

Like many ancient customs whose roots are lost in time there are a variety of theories as to the origins of this particular event, which takes place at the start of the annual Ferry Fair. To some he is a kind of scape-goat. The burrs represent the weight of the sins of his community; burdened with them he is forced to walk this long route, heavily disguised for even his face is covered with green burrs. Like sacrificial offerings, he wears a cap or hat surrounded with roses. He may be a survival of the 'Wicker Men' which the Romans accused the Celtic people of making, which were eventually burned on a great pyre. The Green Man legend has a long history, and many ways of making Green Men are possible, but one which can move on its own feet would be an advantage. Earlier Burry Men were carted about on a hand trolley, or even on horseback.

Some of the tales associated with this interesting old custom relate to the sea, rather than the land, and tell of years when the herring fishing was very poor. In the 1850s or 60s a coastal fisherman was clad in the burrs, in order to bring luck to the nets. Fishermen the world over are very superstitious, and many things can mean ill or good luck in their chancy trade. Perhaps the burrs were to represent the weight of fish to be caught just as securely in the nets. The timing of the procession nowadays suggests it is more likely to be a thanks offering rather than encouragement, as it is at the end of the fishing season. It is about right for the fruit harvest though.

August's Saints

August has a selection of saints who came to particularly sticky ends. St Laurence, whose feast day is 10 August, was a Spanish Deacon who was martyred in AD 258 by being roasted alive on a grid-iron – so now he is the patron of bakers, cooks and pastry chefs. On the thirteenth it is the Feast of St Cassian, whose unpleasant teaching methods applied too vigorously to his pagan pupils led to him being stabbed to death with iron pen nibs by his misused students. As a result of this unpleasant fate he is now the patron saint of

school masters and teachers, which could be even worse!

St Helena, the formidable mother of the Emperor Constantine, is celebrated on the 18 August, and prayers to her are for protection against fire or lightning strikes, which are fairly common about this time of year. Bartlemas or the Feast of St Bartholomew used to be highly riotous when celebrated in London at Smithfield, but it isn't any more. His martyrdom was caused by being skinned alive, and so he is patron saint of butchers, skinners, tanners and bookbinders. At West Witton in North Yorkshire a local custom involves a kind of guy which is paraded through the town. The marchers stop outside houses or pubs to chant a dirge for this much dismembered character who, after a certain amount of community drinking, is taken outside the town, stabbed and finally set on fire. The origins of 'Burning Bartle' are obscure, but it may recall the old tradition of parading saints' effigies around their parish on the feast day, or the even older idea of the sacrificial victim being cast out and eventually destroyed, taking with him the sins of the parishioners.

St John the Baptist was beheaded on 29 August at the request of Herod's dancing girl, Salome, and his head on a dish harks back to the old Celtic legend of Bran, the Sun God and King. Bran was seriously hurt in a battle in Ireland to set free his sister, Branwen, who was wedded to the cruel King of Ireland. He told his followers to cut off his head and keep it, and it told stories for many years. No doubt these two famous heads became united as the Celtic pagan ideas merged with the newer faith, and the Celtic mind linked Salome and Branwen in their tales.

August 15 is the Feast of the Assumption of the Virgin Mary; this is when, her works accomplished on Earth, she was taken up into Heaven. The worship of Mary the Virgin provided a continuing link between the older and very widespread worship of a Goddess who was a Maid, a Mother and a Widow or Old Lady. Many early churches were dedicated in her name, or in that of one of her titles, Mother of Mercy, Star of the Sea, Seat of Wisdom, Gate of Heaven and many other honorifics.

It has always seemed a valuable act of prayer to

light a candle before a holy image. Plump, full-breasted Goddess figures were found in Stone Age cave dwellings, deeply hidden in dark caverns. They were either small figurines or actually carved onto the rock wall, using the natural contours of the stone. Here simple lamps burning fat or oil have also been found; this is clearly an on-going tradition, seen in many Catholic churches to this day.

The Balloon Fiesta

Another, and more mundane way for ordinary mortals to ascend into the heavens is during the Bristol Balloon Fiesta, held early in August, when many hot air balloonists gather for mass ascents, when well over a hundred rainbow coloured balloons, heated by gas burners, heave themselves off the ground like awakening monsters, and drift downwind, at dawn and sunset. During the days in the rolling and wooded grounds of the mansion at Ashton Court, to the west of the city, and quite close to the Avon Gorge and Brunel's delicate suspension bridge, various other aerial displays, microlight planes, helicopters, autogiros and related items are on view. There are long-distance races, where the balloon pilots have to judge the windspeed and direction and height to gain the greatest distance in a given time, and 'Hare and Hound' chases, where one vibrantly coloured balloon is chased across the skies by a pursuing pack. There is something utterly fascinating in the shapes and flights of these lighter-than-air craft, and hearing the roar of their burners and seeing their pear-shaped shadows pass across my window always brings me out to watch.

The Glorious Twelfth

Another activity connected with flying, though with not such lucky consequences as the Hot Air Balloonists, is the shooting of pheasants and grouse after the Glorious Twelfth. Carefully reared birds are harried from their woodlands into the open where 'Guns' do their best to knock them from the sky. The grouse are wilder, living in rough heather moors, which in its own way is just as carefully farmed as the smooth sheep pastures. Although the coppices have to be kept wild, and undisturbed by casual walkers, much of the wildlife that lives there, the foxes, the crows, the stoats or weasels, perhaps even the badgers, tend to fall foul of the gamekeepers and end up dead and exhibited along any barbed wire fence which is convenient.

Renting out shoots does undoubtedly make money for the landowners; it occupies the Gamekeepers all year, and brings profit to the beaters, loaders, dog trainers and their wives, who produce sumptuous portable banquets to be consumed during lulls in the shoot. There are probably other 'psychological' aspects, in that the natural desire to hunt and kill things to eat is part of our genetic makeup, although not that many women actually take to the Butts, or if they do, it is not to shoot. Although organised Game Shoots require very little in the nature of stalking and getting downwind of your prey, when the birds are actually beaten out of cover so that they fly at a convenient height in front of the Butts, hitting them does require skill, but no doubt so does hitting Clay Pigeons, which you cannot eat.

LEO, THE LION

Perhaps the hunting spirit of August has something to do with its sign of the zodiac, Leo the Lion, although it is the lionesses who do most of the work while their menfolk lie about the veldt looking elegant. Leo is ruled by the Sun, and so it is an outgoing, bright and cheerful part of the zodiac. Leos are often leaders, whether on a world scale, or as chairpersons of village committees. They are great organisers, very generous with their time, money, resources and hospitality, in a good cause. Those born between about 22 July and 21 August will often be lion-like in their natures, and some of them will undoubtedly have real manes of thick and wavy hair. Many are cat as opposed to dog-lovers, and have many feline traits in their make-up.

As the Sun in astrology relates to the personality, Leos are very direct people. Their self-confidence and drive will help them shine in any situation, and their openness and fair dealing will make them popular as arbiters in local disputes. Some are very thoughtful so their opinions are perceived by others as valuable, though they can be forceful in getting their own way, and could be seen as domineering or arrogant.

Within their family they are much liked, but sometimes they may have no children, or sadly lose their children through illness or accident. However, they overcome this sort of sadness through their friends and business contacts. They usually have great senses of humour and are fun-loving, generous to a fault, and voluble, although their inner natures are gentle and peaceful, prefering a quiet life, like that of their Leonine fellow creatures.

Leos can be very ambitious, and they can pursue ideals or objectives to a bitter end. They are no good at diplomacy or anything which might hint at double-dealing, for they are naturally direct and open in all their dealings, hating lies or deceit. They love comfort and luxury and have ways of making their surroundings appear rich, even if they are managing on a tight budget. They make devoted and loyal companions, but can be lazy, or overbearing and arrogant if they feel they are being thwarted in their desires.

The colours which Leos like include the most vibrant golds and yellows, brilliant and even clashing colours, like orange with bright blue, or lime green. They often love gold or gold-coloured jewellery and make their homes glitter with polished brass or copper, reflecting great bunches of brilliant flowers. They often like to be in the open air, but prefer gardens to wooded glades or riverside walks. Many are excellent gardeners, typically preferring great sunflowers or bright clusters of larger flowers to the delicate tracery of small blooms. The jewels which are particularly attractive to these out-going people include amber, tourmaline, topaz, sardonyx, chrysolite and some rubies. They prefer gold settings, but all lavish and decorative pieces will appeal to their sense of beauty.

Famous people born under the sign of Leo include Napoleon Bonaparte, and Benito Mussolini who shared his birthday with Rasputin, but they have literary talents among them as shown by George Bernard Shaw, Sir Walter Scott, the poet Shelley, and Alexandre Dumas. Dr Carl Jung was a Leo; Princess Anne, the Princess Royal, is, and so is the early astronaut, Neil Armstrong.

August Recipes

Real Lemonade

Garnished with a few mint leaves or a slice of fresh lemon, this is the ideal drink for a hot day.

3 or 4 lemons
4 oz/125g/½ cup sugar
1½ pints/90cl/4 cups boiling water

Wash the lemons, squeeze out as much juice as you can, and remove the zest from the rinds. Put the zest and sugar into a large jug, pour over the boiling water and allow to cool before adding the lemon juice. Chill the lemonade before serving.

Gingerbread Men

Wakes Weeks were often marked by the visit of a fair where, as well as the various side-shows, there would traditionally be stalls selling 'fairings' – cakes and biscuits – to sustain the revellers. Gingerbread men have always been favourite fairings, both with adults and children.

8 oz/250g plain flour
4 oz/125g butter
4 oz/125g sugar
2 tbsp treacle
2 tsp ground ginger
1 tsp ground cinnamon
1 tsp bicarbonate of soda

Mix the dry ingredients. Warm the butter, sugar and treacle over a low heat, stirring continuously, until melted. Allow to cool, then pour into the dry ingredients. Mix thoroughly, then roll out thinly and cut into 'man' shapes. Decorate with currants for faces and eyes. Bake in a moderate oven, 180°C/350°F/Gas Mark 4, for about 15 minutes.

Flowerpot Bread

Lammas Day, 1 August, is named from the Old English Hlafmas or loaf mass, at which the bread made from the first of the harvest was eaten and dedicated to the Gods. For an unusual lammas loaf why not try 'flowerpot bread' where the loaf is baked in a clay flowerpot. Earthenware pots were used to baking long before tins were used, and are said to retain the bread's rich flavour, as well as giving an unusual and attractively shaped loaf. Obviously you will want to use new pots for baking. Grease them well and bake them empty in a hot oven before use. Any favourite bread recipe can be used. The following recipe uses a mix of wholemeal and white flour.

½ oz/15g fresh yeast
½ pint/30cl lukewarm milk and water
½ lb/250g wholemeal flour
½ lb/250g strong white flour
1 tsp salt

Dissolve the yeast in ¼ pint of warm milk and water, and leave in a warm place for ten minutes or until frothy. Put the flours and salt in a large bowl, make a well in the centre, and pour in the yeast mixture together with the rest of the milk/water. Mix well until a soft dough is formed, then knead on a floured board for 10–15 minutes. Put the dough into a greased bowl, cover with a damp cloth, and leave to rise in a warm place until doubled in bulk (about one hour). Knead the dough again for 5–10 minutes, then put into a well-greased 2 lb loaf tin. Leave in a warm place until the dough has risen to the top of the tin, then bake in a hot oven (225°C/425°F/Mark 7) for 30–40 minutes.

HOW TO MAKE CORN DOLLIES

Corn Dollies are an excellent way of celebrating the harvest and they can be used to decorate a special table or festive meal. The simplest one is made of a small sheaf of stalks of corn, wrapped in a handkerchief or a cone-shaped dress of flowery material, so that the ears of corn make a head and hands. Sometimes just a bunch of corn bound with red ribbons is sufficient.

If you want to make a woven Corn Dolly you will need some long stems of wheat or oats which should be stripped of any leaves and wrapped in a damp cloth for a while. Taking five stalks, bind them together and begin weaving the square shape typical of many such dolls by crossing straw 1 over straws 2 and 3, then crossing the straw immediately to the left of the straw just moved over the next two straws – so straw 3 would be crossed over straws 1 and 4, then straw 4 would be crossed over straws 3 and 5 – and so on, making the square spread out and form the typical spiral of 'corners'. You can learn the technique with pipe cleaners, and once you have the basic art, it can be applied to rushes, lavender stems or any other kinds of flexible stems of grass or flowers. To join straws, do so at a corner by inserting the thinner end of a new straw into that which has run out, and folding the next straw over the join.

Some Corn Dollies are made over a core of shaped straws, often with nice ears of corn. These designs may be huge, or tiny, and are found from Guatemala to Greece, in regional variations. They are usually bound with red ribbon or red wool to hold the final ends in place, and to make a loop for hanging the completed dolly up.

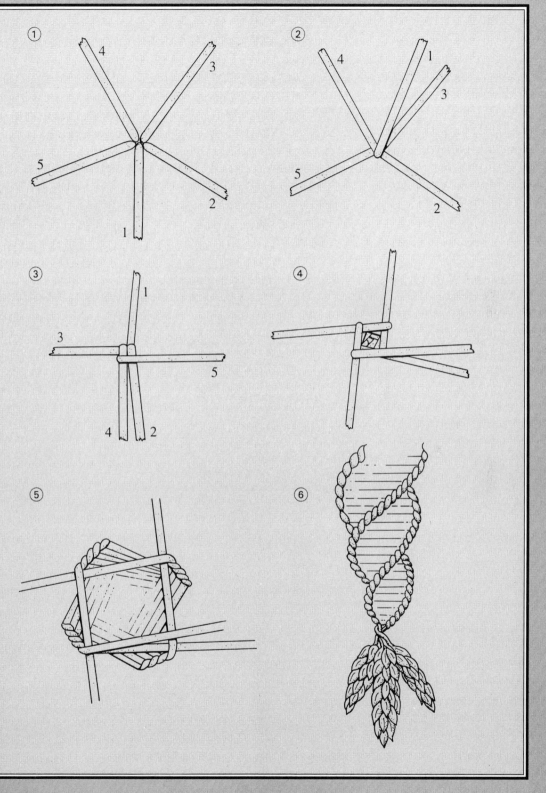

AUGUST SONG

John Barleycorn

There was three men came out of the west,
Their fortunes for to try,
And these three men made a solemn vow,
John Barleycorn should die.
They ploughed, they sowed, they harrowed
   him in,
Throwed clods upon his head,
And these three men made a solemn vow,
John Barleycorn was dead.

Then they let him lie for a very long time
Till the rain from heaven did fall,
Then little Sir John sprung up his head,
And soon amazed them all.
They let him stand till midsummer
Till he looked both pale and wan,
And little Sir John he growed a long beard
And so became a man.

They hired men with the scythes so sharp
To cut him off at the knee,
They rolled him and tied him by the waist,
And served him most barbarously.
They hired men with the sharp pitchforks
Who pricked him to the heart,
And the loader he served him worse than that,
For he bound him to the cart.

They wheeled him round and round the field
Till they came unto a barn,
And there they made a solemn mow
Of poor John Barleycorn.
They hired men with the crab-tree sticks
To cut him skin from bone,
And the miller he served him worse than that,
For he ground him between two stones.

Here's little Sir John in a nut-brown bowl,
And brandy in a glass;
And little Sir John in the nut-brown bowl
Proved the stronger man at last.
And the huntsman he can't hunt the fox,
Nor so loudly blow his horn,
And the tinker he can't mend kettles or pots
Without a little of Barleycorn.

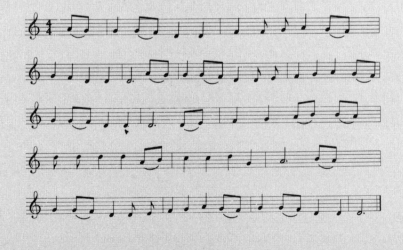

94

SEPTEMBER

Next him, September marched eke on foote,
Yet was he heavy laden with the spoyle
Of harvests riches, which he made his booty,
And him enricht with bounty of the soyle.

Edmund Spenser: *'The VII Booke of the Faerie Queene'*

September is a time of gathering, not only the obvious bounty of the countryside, but of our own achievements. It has the feeling of an ending, and though in some lands and faiths September actually brings in the New Year, it has a feeling of fullness and completion. That is largely how our rural ancestors felt. In earlier times it signified the end of the corn, oats and barley harvest, with all the work of threshing still to follow. But it also brought forth new harvests, from orchard and field, from hedgerow and coppice. We are so used to our fruits and vegetables coming to us in neat plastic packages, brightly wrapped on the supermarket shelves, or tossed in haphazard piles on market stalls, that we often forget the trees which gave our apples and pears, our plums and peaches their birth and nurture.

We need to learn anew the sources of our food, where it grew, how it was nursed into ripeness, how it was picked, preserved and transported. The time has gone by when we can no longer care nor require to know. The world is changing at a great rate, and all our activities are being weighed and reconsidered for the first time in history. Humanity is seeing the other side of the plentiful harvests it has demanded. The hardwoods which look so beautiful in our homes are not being replaced once they are cut. The cheap potatoes, the bread flour, much of which is expensively imported from America or Canada, the over-protected field crops with all their need for fertilisers, insecticides and weed killers; all these are taking a great toll from the very soil in which they grow. Many leave a bitter aftertaste of spent chemicals, soil erosion and polluted streams, from which our own drinking water may be drawn. Harvest used to be a time of reward, of fulfilment; now there is a darker shadow hanging over all we grow and consume. The more we learn about the real costs of things the more clearly we will be able to understand how folly, greed and expediency in the past have left a blighted harvest.

This used to be a time of great rejoicing, celebration and contentment because the hardworking and humble country folk held their land in reverence. They treated the fields as well as they could, caring for the soil, the livestock, the hedges and the wildlife, for all were seen as part of the pattern. They took their calendar from the moon's phases, knowing instinctively when something needed doing, or when something was going wrong. The arrival of spring migrants told them when to sow, the departure of the same birds showed them when to gather in the natural harvests from the wild. They felt they were part of the land, wedded to it as were the kings of old to their realms. There was a religious aspect to all this, a feeling of harmony and respect. Mechanisation has put an end to that.

But even if we can't share that ancient bond with the Earth, we can start to recognise that times, places and activities can be by their own nature holy and, by celebrating that discovery, we may find a way of restoring the health both to the people, many of whom will have to admit they are not one hundred per cent well and happy, and to the land. It is not necessary to acknowledge a Mother Nature or Earth Goddess if that is contrary to your feelings, but simply to sense the fulfilment of the Harvest Festival in church, the wealth of berries free for the gathering in many a hedgerow, the colour in a ripe apple, the flavour of a ripe fruit in your mouth, and a thanksgiving in your heart, if not on your lips, for that experience. Harvest is an especially important season in this respect.

Rosh Hashanah

September to the Jewish community is the New Year, *Rosh Hashanah*, celebrated at the New Moon. To these people it is a time of new beginnings, the wearing of new clothes and of New Year Greetings. It is also a time of soul-searching and repentance, and traditionally sins were cast out into running water or into the original 'scapegoat', after which the animal was set free in the desert, having been dedicated to the demon 'Azazel', the Sin Bearer. It is a time for public rather than private prayers, in contrast to most Jewish ritual, which takes place in the home. The *shofar*, a ram's horn trumpet, is sounded, and there are ten days of penitence and meditation on the power of God. On the tenth day of the *Tishri* (September moon) falls the Festival of *Yom Kippur*, the Day of Atonement. It is the Sabbath of Sabbaths, and a day of great purification, repentance and prayers for regeneration. Prayers for the dead are also said, hymns are sung, and memorial candles are lit. At the end of a day spent in fasting and prayer, the *shofar* is again sounded and the fast is ended. Many of these ancient traditions exist in the way modern pagans celebrate Harvest tide.

Abbots Bromley Horn Dance

One of the most spectacular English ceremonies is the Abbots Bromley Horn Dance, which takes place on the Monday, following the Sunday after 4 September. Early on that morning the sets of ancient reindeer horns are brought out from the parish church, each attached to a miniature deer's head and a pole by which the dancers carry these heavy tributes. Half the sets are painted white, the other half have gold tips to the antlers. There is a Maid Marian – a man dressed as a woman, a Hobby Horse, a Fool or Jester and a boy with a

bow and arrow, and two musicians, one nowadays with an accordian and a boy with a triangle. A series of interwoven steps with ten dancers in a line is followed by the formation of a circle, and then the teams of dancers skip off in opposite directions. The stag dance follows when the dancers with antlers mime the fighting clash of rutting stags, advancing and retreating three times. The other characters snap their sticks or bows or bang a ladle in time to the music, which now is a variety of folk tunes, because the original 'genuine' Horn Dance tune was lost at the end of the 1880s. The dancers meet and cross over three times and 'fight' three times, then form a line and continue on their way, repeating the pattern countless times during a long day of dancing.

Dressed in muted colours, the team of

extremely strong dancers, with their medieval costumes, flat caps and hard shoes, tramp their stately paces through the streets until evening. As wild deer are just beginning to fight the dance may simply reflect a fertility theme, but old records seem to indicate that originally the ritual was performed at Christmas or New Year. The character of the 'man-woman' or Maid Marian is a common one in Mumming Plays, again usually associated with Yuletide, and the archer with his bow may suggest a hunting theme. All these old rites are intended to bring good luck, fertility, health and success to all who attend them, and perhaps casting a few coins in the Maid's ladle will bring extra benefit! The strange, potent atmosphere that such antique dances generate is not found in ordinary events or pastimes.

Fish and Oyster Harvests

Other kinds of harvests have their festivals in September – fish and oysters. As September is the first month since April with an 'R' in it, oysters are again in season, and the oyster fisheries, particularly in Essex, have a celebration now. Pollution has taken its toll of these tasty delicacies, which only a few hundred years ago were so cheap they were a staple food of people living near the Thames or other rivers in which they lived. In Roman times they were greatly appreciated, and most of the sites of that period excavated by archaeologists turn up piles of the discarded, undecayed shells. Other oysters which attracted the Romans to Britain contain a dark red or purple dye, used to edge the togas of officials and important people in far away Rome.

In several parts of Scotland, around Musselburgh in Midlothian, they celebrate the Fishermen's Walk. The fishing fleet is all in harbour and the houses are decorated with flags and flowers. Some women dress in traditional costume and carry a large doll or effigy through the streets. At the end of the Walk there are sports and games.

These games are not the same as the various lots of Highland Games, which take place throughout the summer with a collection of specifically Scottish competitions. These include Tossing the Caber, a tree trunk nearly twenty feet long, thrown so that it flies through the air in an arc. It should land in a line with the 'tosser' and the winner is he who throws it the furthest. Other traditional games, which must date back a long way, involve throwing very heavy boulders of rock, 'Throwing the Hammer', an iron ball on a chain, as well as running and hurdle races. One of these at the Fort Williams Games, in July,

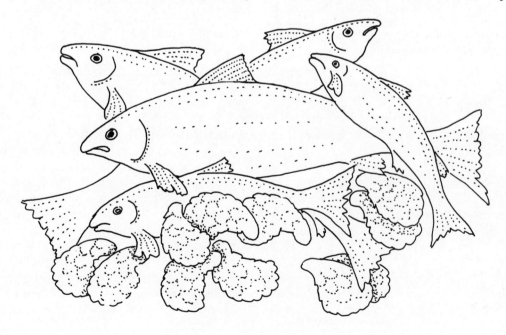

involves running up and down the mountain, Ben Nevis, over a thirteen mile course.

The Wild Harvest

Gathering the wild harvests which have been ripening all through the summer reaches a climax, in most years, in September. There are all kinds of berries, blackberries being the most common, and the most widely used for pies, jam, wine and cordials. Also collected are rosehips, from the wild rose; sloes to make not only sloe gin, but healing potions, whortleberries from the moors, again for jam or jelly; rowan berries, haws, wild damsons and many of the vast bounty of the hedgerows. Where there is unpolluted and relatively traffic-free access to these fruits, it used to be customary for whole families equipped with hooked sticks and flat baskets to roam the lanes and fields, where the farmer gave permission, to gather huge quantities of these naturally grown, organic and healing fruits, but today it is less common. I even heard a mother scolding a child who was reaching for a ripe, cultivated blackberry hanging over a garden fence, 'Don't eat those poison berries!'

There are many mushrooms and toadstools which in other parts of Europe form an autumnal feast, yet in the British woodlands, except for the intervention of a few enthusiasts, these fungi are left to the mice and insects to devour. There are very few actually poisonous mushrooms to be found in our wastelands, although there are lots which are not worth eating because they have no real flavour. However the fragrant peach scent of a freshly picked chanterelle, the sweet, firm flesh of a large puffball, or the nutty taste of a boletus fried in bacon fat is a delight to any peasant's palate. In France, Italy and Poland whole holidays are devoted to tracking down the many varieties of woodland and field fungi which are used immediately in delightful seasonal dishes, such as omelettes and savoury starters, as freshly picked as can be. In Japan, logs are specially placed so that they can rot and produce the Shitaki mushroom, which we import in its dried form, but some of these are being cultivated in the same way in British woodlands. We are very

unadventurous on the fungi front, and many people are actually still suspicious of the safe and relatively tasteless cultivated mushrooms, let alone the smokey wood mushrooms making a rare appearance on the greengrocer's shelves. One of the fungi to avoid is the fungus so often depicted in Fairy Stories, the *Amanita muscaria*, or Fly Agaric, with its brilliant red cap with white spots. That is *not* to be sampled.

At the end of the last century the hop fields of Kent rang with the cries of the vast army of labourers who had quit London to pull the bines and strip their loads of rustling green cones. This task is now performed by loud machines, and many of the hops which give English beer its characteristic bitter taste come in from Germany. The scent of hops often found straying along hedgerows is wonderful, a combination of a sharp lemony smell with a deeper spicy, peppery undertone. As well as being a vital ingredient in real beer, they have always been used in herbal pillows to bring sleep and peace to those who suffer restless nights.

Another harvest at this time of year, more of interest to urban children than rural folk, are the horse chestnuts, or 'conkers'. These beautiful, glossy brown fruits in their green and spikey cases have fascinated generations of youngsters, who as soon as any are seen to fall from the trees, as Nature intended, are out there with heavy sticks, becoming a hazard to traffic and passers-by, by 'throwing up for conkers' in order to knock down the largest ones. Taking their haul home and begging an old fashioned meat skewer, or its

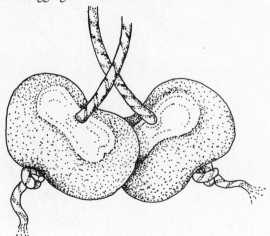

modern equivalent, they will pierce the best conkers and thread a string with a large knot at the end through it. They then need an opponent to conquer. By taking alternate turns the players strike at each others' conkers by holding the nut in one hand and a reefed length of string in the other and making a sharp, downward strike, aiming at the weak spot near the string hole, in order to smash the opponent's conker to pieces. The winner of this contest is then able to call his conker a 'One-er', having broken one other conker, but if his victim had been a 'fiver' or whatever, his would become that number, plus one. It made a certain amount of skulduggery inevitable, baking the conkers or soaking them in special potions to make them harder, so that it was possible to end up with a battered but un-broken 'hundred-and-tenner' or more.

The girls, at this time, having more care for their bruised fingers which inevitably get in the way of flying conkers, use these same nuts to make furniture for a doll's house. Using pins and coloured wool, they make chairs or tables, and by adding other sorts of seeds, such as acorns and their cups, beechmast with their prickly three-sided shells, the winged seeds of sycamore, honesty and small birds' feathers, they make miniature dolls, animals or decorations, which later on, sprayed with silver or gold paint, might reappear on the Christmas Tree. They can be hung from a wire frame to make a mobile, or from a whitewashed branch of a tree to be an autumnal arrangement, along with branches of hips and scarlet haws. Some of these fruit-rich branches can be cut and fixed near a window so that the birds can feed during colder weather, and those in the warmth of the house can enjoy watching their activities in comfort.

The Meaning of Harvest

Other displays of fruits and vegetables may be found at the end of September in the parish churches, who sometimes celebrate Harvest Festival around this time. It used to be an opportunity to offer the biggest, ripest, most polished produce from the vegetable garden or allotment; now it is more often shop-bought and even foreign produce that is donated. Oranges and bananas are hardly an English Harvest, although those huge marrows, far too tough to eat (although they can produce wonderful Marrow Rum) and sheafs of corn and baskets of mixed fruits, scrubbed potatoes, vast green cabbages and white curded cauliflowers should all have a place of offering before the altar, if they have been anointed with the sweat of your brow, and the concern in your heart.

We, who only see the countryside through a car window, will all sing 'We plough the fields and scatter...' or 'All is safely gathered in...' with vigour, even though our own harvest has been a single sprig of parsley from the windowbox!

Perhaps our own real harvests have been a job completed, another book written, a contract fulfilled, a computer program sorted out, a house repainted and filled with beautiful things. A garden recreated out of wilderness or builders' rubble offers a harvest, as does any act of restoration, be it antique furniture or the state of your soul. Try to gain an insight into the true inner meaning of harvest, which is completion, and gathering in, and then the final phase – the sorting out and setting aside the 'seeds' for next year's harvest, projects or accomplishments. It is a time of casting out; like the Spring Cleaning season in February, harvest time expects us to examine our neglected drawers and overflowing cupboards. We have to cast away husks, unfinished works, the dregs of things we will never complete, and this is hard. The farmer faces the same dilemma; which of his beasts to send to slaughter, which pieces of equipment cannot go one more season, which crops to abandon, which fields to cultivate and which to set aside for grass. It is all a part of the great pattern, and can be a fulfilling experience when it is done.

Autumnal Equinox

There is a festival in mid September, forgotten by most people who do not have a solar-orientated calendar for it is the Day of the Autumnal Equinox, when day and night are equal again, and the setting of the sun, when it is visible in many of the rings of standing stones, falls in a preset slot, exactly marking time. Many of the new pagan groups, who celebrate all the old feast days, have included it in their cycle of rituals, and see it as a time of balance and reflection. It is when the Lord of the Sky and Wildlife withdraws into his winter self, returning to the Underworld wherein those who have died rest, and those who are yet to be born prepare for incarnation. Like the Egyptian God, Osiris, with his green face, he represents the power of the seed, buried in the soil, but not yet visible. He is potential, hope and the promise of the return to light and life in due season. Those who follow these restored old ways use this time now to balance their inner and outer lives, sorting and selecting those things to be replanted, and those

to be cast aside. It is a time of both physical and mental recycling, and an important turning point in the life of the soul. Some of the modern Druid groups also celebrate at this time, acknowledging the harvest of field and hand, and climbing a sacred hill to bid the summer sun farewell.

Widecombe Fair

One folk song which is familiar to many is 'Widecombe Fair':

Tom Pearce, Tom Pearce, Lend me your grey mare,
All along, out along, down along lea,
For I want to go to Widecombe Fair,
With Bill Brewer, Jan Stewer, Peter Gurney, Dan'l Widdon, Harry Hawke,
Old Uncle Tom Cobley and all, Old Uncle Tom Cobley and all!

This Fair, held on a Tuesday in September, was originally a gathering of the Dartmoor ponies, who were driven into this small town set deep in a valley on the moor. Widecombe Fair doesn't have such a long history as many of the other autumnal gatherings, but it is famous because of its song. Now it consists almost entirely of a Fun Fair with sideshows and stalls selling commodities, although there is a little sheep and horse dealing still done. Sadly many of the wild Dartmoor ponies don't become delightful rides for pony-mad children. They are more likely to end up on the dinner tables of France and Belgium as prime, organic horseflesh. There are just too many half-wild ponies for them all to be taken up by riding schools and private buyers, and, anyway, having grown up on the unfenced moors, to bring them into stables, break them to the saddle and make them obedient to riders can sometimes be a long and difficult task. Many ponies are killed or maimed by cars which drive on all the narrow, twisting moorland lanes, as are sheep and the cattle grazed by common right on the heathery hills.

Visitors to Dartmoor or the New Forest where ponies, cattle and sheep roam free can help by driving with extra care. They should also refrain from feeding livestock as it encourages them to expect food from cars.

Michaelmas

Michaelmas, on 29 September, the Feast Day of St Michael, Archangel and caster-out of Satan, dragon combatant, and patron of soldiers, horses and high places, used to be a great Feast. Its main dish was usually goose, fattened on the stubble and fallen grain in the cornfields. Their pecking for insects, their trampling down the stubble, eating of the weeds and grasses below the corn, and their fertility-restoring droppings would all go to improve the field for next year's crop. They would then produce a fine, fat carcass, just the right size for a family celebration dinner. Geese have always been part of the traditional farmyard scene, and long ago they were used as 'guard birds' because their fierceness and loud voices were an excellent deterrent to both two-footed and four-footed raiders in the henhouse. A large gander would take on anyone, and his great wings are plenty strong enough to break a man's arm if he tackled these protective birds on their own territory.

St Michael no longer has a fixed kind of celebration, however, nor do any of the towns which have their principal church dedicated to him appear to have a shared tradition. But, as a character who took over many of the roles of the previous Sun God, his feast day must have been an important one. A recent body of research is demonstrating that the many hilltop churches dedicated to this flying saint are aligned with each other. Some of them, like that on the top of St Michael's Mount, an island off Cornwall (well, it is an island at high tide!), the one on Glastonbury Tor, and one on Brentor in Devon, where there has been a church on a high and lonely peak since AD 1130, were never in places especially accessible to the parishioners expected to worship there. They were, however, in just the right place to connect with the two older powers, of Earth and Sky. As obvious resting places for the Sun and Sky God such heights were ideal, and as wild uninhabited places they were also the last refuges of the Old Mother Goddess. From these rocky interconnections flowed the fertile current, depicted all over the world as a Dragon, Serpent or Worm, whose magical green blood flowed as life in the verdant mantle of the fields. Perhaps these dragon fights were not so much the Archangel destroying an evil beast, but rather a shepherd of Power directing the energy which flows down from these high places, like a dam in a river, so that the benefit is sent where it is most needed.

All over the world ancient sites are being re-examined, and in many of them there is a carving, mound, reshaped river or some other sinuous construction which relates to this Serpentine life-force. Many of these sites are also found on the same Great Circles which can be drawn around a globe, as straight 'leylines' can be drawn on a flat map. What may be being discovered is that certain places have always been sacred, and it is this presence of sacredness that has caused the building of holy structures on that ground. Nowadays, of course, most people are only aware of the structures. The erection of churches, circles or patterns of standing stones, pyramids, temples, Holy Cities, like Mecca or Jerusalem, or Zimbabwe or Palenque, or many of the oldest religious constructions all have that same underlying sacredness, upon which their later worshippers have created shrines.

There are two sorts of sacredness: one is of

place and its associations, with a great Teacher, perhaps, or a religious event, which may well predate whatever monument is upon the place now; and the other is the sacredness of Time. That is a frozen moment when a certain revivifying power can be apprehended by those awakened to that force, which occurs as the turning seasons cycle round their perpetual way. Michaelmas with its many forgotten rituals and ceremonies is certainly about this same process. It would be a blessing to revive the old Feast when the huge white birds, which also guarded the holy places as well as the Celtic farmsteads, were eaten; when the hazels on the diviner's magic bushes ripened, to feed the legendary Salmon of Wisdom in their pool, and feed the people wisdom also. Apples could be picked now from the Celtic Tree of Immortality, whose flowering branch would be a passport into Fairyland and a safe return.

When you walk in a garden or park and see the first hint of autumn in the air, smell the purple spikes of Michaelmas daisies, with their spicey scent, notice the scarlet bunches of fruits on the Guelder Rose drooping amid leaves turning crimson and gold, ask a blessing. When your basket is heavy with the joyful feast of blackberries, or hips or juniper berries to flavour gin, or any other of this season's harvest, breathe a small prayer to Michael the Victorious, in these words, from the Gaelic:

Thou, Michael the Victorious, I make my circuit
   under thy shield.
Thou, Michael of the white steed, And of the
   bright and brilliant blade!
Conqueror of the Dragon, Be thou at my back.
Thou ranger of the heavens; Thou warrior of the
   King of all!
Thou, Michael the Victorious – My pride and my
   guide!
Thou, Michael the Victorious, The Glory of mine
   eye!

It is especially valuable if you are feeling glum or sad because the light of summer is fading. Think that the light is sinking within you, and that the warmth of the summer sun will burn in your heart, even if it is not visible in the sky.

Sacred Yew Trees

Wherever you travel around Britain, if you visit old churches you will often come upon ancient Yew Trees, either singly or in avenues. Recent research has dated many of these vast, slow growing evergreens to over a thousand years old. Some, indeed, are more than two thousand years old, long predating the church which has been constructed in their shadow.

At Painswick in Gloucestershire, on 19th September, which is the Feast of the Nativity of St Mary in the old calendar, there is a custom of 'Clipping the Church'. In part this is concerned with giving the ancient churchyard yews their annual haircut, and in part it is concerned with the parishioners actually, physically, embracing their church. This kind of activity takes place at other times of year in different places, but always involves the entire congregation gathering to encircle the church, singing hymns, and showing their care.

Traditionally the Yew is the Tree of Eternity, outliving the sacred oaks and the mighty ash trees by hundreds of years. The Druids were aware of this record longevity and probably held court under the spreading, evergreen branches. In some cases early churches had to be built over the roots of already well established yew trees. They are found in the grounds of ancient abbeys, and sometimes stand in places from which all traces of the building, which in Saxon times was often of wooden construction, have long since disappeared. It is only the positions of ancient yews, standing to the sides of the site, which have led archaeologists to re-discover the foundations of such ancient Christian places of worship. Many such archaic chapels were sacred to the Druids long before the arrival of the Christian message, and it is in their honour that the tree was deliberately planted. Under their shade are places where ritual and celebration has been carried on for perhaps three thousand years, and they need preservation, protection and to be kept free of strangling ivy so that they may continue for, perhaps, another thousand years.

VIRGO, THE VIRGIN

Most of September is under the domain of Virgo, the Eternal Virgin who ascended into Heaven in the previous month. She is also Ceres, the Plentiful Corn Goddess, Lady of Cereals, who offers her sheaf of ripe corn to the people. In British folklore she has come to us as Mother Carey, whose manifold chickens are all kinds of wild birds, particularly sea birds. She is a Somerset river too, and part of her curving course outlines the figure of Virgo in the Glastonbury Earth Zodiac. Here it passes through the village of Babcary, an easy place to enter but a hard one to get out of. This Virgo is pregnant, and her swollen belly and full breast is outlined by a winding waterway. Upon her breast is Wimble Toot, with an earthwork forming her nipple.

People born under the stars of the heavenly Virgo, between about 22 August and 21 September, are adaptable, and their care for detail ensures they will be at home with the complex technologies and computer applications. They will enjoy the solo effort involved in this kind of work, too, for they are not natural 'joiners'. Being governed by Mercury they are good at communication, research and mathematics, but they may have a heartless streak, for their emotions are deeply buried, and they like to succeed. They prefer ordered and elegant surroundings, and in extreme cases can be pernickety and perfectionists of the highest order, making them trying bosses and infuriating partners in any enterprise. They could be careful pharmacists or chemists, politicians determined to get to the bottom of matters, accountants and auditors, lawyers and detectives.

As the summer draws to its end there is always a time of introspection which is very much part of the Virgoan character. These people, often rather slender in build, with thin faces showing excellent bone structure, like to organise and tidy things up. September is the natural time for this. Although some are shy in their dealings with others they are interested in both things and people, but their constant quest for knowledge, information or explanations can bring them to the forefront of their particular subject, as researchers, scientists or acknowledged experts.

Some are drawn to teaching, though their ideas or methods may be seen as unorthodox or innovative. They are hard task-masters, expecting the same high degree of accuracy and care that they find natural to apply to any process. Some can be eccentric or hold unlikely views or opinions, or give the impression the are prejudiced or hyper-critical, making them hard to please. They also tend not to show emotion, being restrained and conservative when not showing those flashes of scientific brilliance they can be capable of.

Colours which will usually appeal to them include most shades of blue, pale turquoise and jade. Muted golds and earthy colours with some warmth suit them, though the brilliant hues which some signs can wear with impunity look terrible on Virgoans. The jewels they prefer include jade, jasper, cornelians, agates and diamonds, especially those in tiny, elegant settings. Lilies and cornflowers are their flowers, and a tree associated with the sign, whose nuts are ripening in their month, is the hazel. They would probably make good water diviners and users of a pendulum for finding things.

September Recipes

Cig Moch a Brithyll (Bacon and Trout)

4 medium-sized trout
8 rashers streaky bacon
salt and pepper
1 tsp butter

Clean the fish and remove the bones. Grease an oven-proofed dish and line the base with half of the bacon rashers. Place the trout on top and cover them with the remaining bacon. Season the fish with salt and pepper and dot with the butter. Bake them in a 425°C/220°F/Mark 7 oven for 20 minutes.

Cottage Cider

As there are usually plenty of apples to be had about now, it is worth making some cider. This is a recipe for old-fashioned cider, which contains raisins.

12 lbs/5.5kg/45 cups (prepared weight) sweet and sour apples
8 pints/5 litres/10 US pints warmed water
1 lb/500g/3 cups raisins, chopped
1½ lb/750g/3 cups sugar
2 tsp wine yeast, dissolved in a little warm water

Wash the apples, then mince or crush them. (A heavy hammer and a clean sack will do the job!) Put the pulp into a wine-making bucket, and add the warmed water, the raisins, sugar and activated yeast. Stir well and cover the bucket, then leave in a warm place for two weeks, stirring and mixing the pulp thoroughly each day. After this time, strain the liquid through double layers of muslin, squeezing out as much juice as possible, into a fermentation jar, and allow to ferment to a finish. Transfer the jar to a cooler place for a month, before syphoning into bottles. As this is a sparkling drink, strong beer or cider bottles with tight fitting stoppers are necessary. It continues to improve with keeping.

Charoseth

This is an apple dish of Jewish extraction, made with eating apples, chopped almonds, sultanas and cinnamon. To each finely grated apple add a teaspoon of chopped almonds and two teaspoons of sultanas and mix well. Make the mixture into small balls by pressing with the fingers, then dust these with a little sugar if necessary and cinnamon to taste.

Blackberry Fool

This is a delicately flavoured, purple-coloured dessert.

About 1 lb/500g/4 cups ripe blackberries
sugar to taste
½ pint/30cl/1⅓ cups double cream
dash blackberry-flavoured liqueur (optional)

Lighly simmer the blackberries in a little water for about ten minutes. Press the purée through a sieve to extract the juice, then sweeten the purée if you feel it is necessary. Whip the cream stiffly and fold it into the purée. If you like, stir in the liqueur.

Hedgerow Jam

1 lb/500g blackberries
1 lb/500g elderberries
8 oz/250g sloes
8 oz/250g rosehips
4 oz/125g haws
4 oz/125g rowan berries
1 lb/500g crab apples, cooking apples or windfalls
6 lb/3kg sugar

Simmer the cleaned, chopped fruit in 2 pints of water for about one hour, or until soft. Add the sugar and simmer, stirring frequently, until the sugar has dissolved. Boil until setting point is reached. Pour into warm jars and cover.

HOW TO MAKE AN EYE OF LIGHT

These ancient symbols, often seen in Mexico, are thought to bring Luck and Harmony wherever they are hung; they also ward off misfortune. To make ordinary small ones, up to about 8 inches (20 centimetres), you need two small sticks of about this length and lots of coloured thick wool, or narrow strips cut from cloth or plastic. First tie the two sticks into an equal-armed cross, then with red or another bright colour begin at the centre winding the wool over each arm of the cross in turn. The strands of wool do not need to be too close together (Fig 1) and changes of colour should be used to make contrasting bands out almost to the ends of the sticks. Finish off with pompoms or tassels of multi-coloured wool on the ends of three of the arms and a loop at the top to hang the decoration up with (Fig 2).

Really large ones, up to a yard (metre) or more across, can be made with strong garden canes and strips of plastic bags stuck together into long ribbons, or with actual ribbons, as outdoor decorations, or party favours. Competitions to make the most neat or colourful Eye of Light symbols could be run.

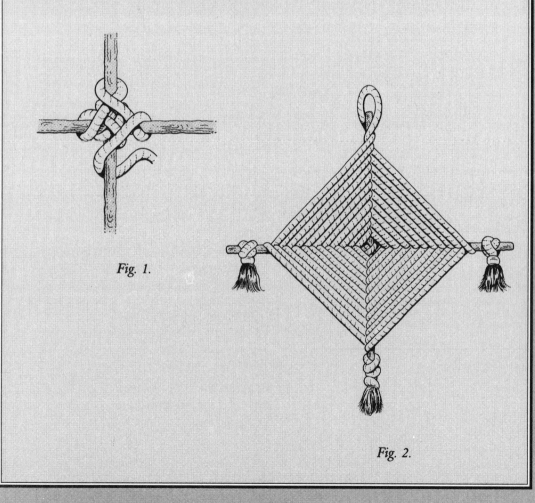

Fig. 1.

Fig. 2.

OCTOBER

October is the fallen leaf, but it is also a wider horizon more clearly seen. It is the distant hills once more in sight, and the enduring constellations above them once again.

Hal Borland: *'Sundial of the Seasons'*

To many people, October is a time of reflection and anxiety, for it is the undoubted end of summer, which often manages to linger on into September. It can feel like a time of decay, of disillusion and of death of Nature. Yet, as far as Nature itself is concerned, it is a time of richness and plenty, of renewal and fertility. The wild fruits, hips, haws, berries and seeds are all falling to earth, to feed the small creatures, to nourish the soil with their soft fleshy parts, and to sow their seeds for the next cycle. Birds thrive on them, and as the leaves fall from the trees and hedges those rarer seed eaters can be seen, and the antics of the common tits, blackbirds and starlings can provide hours of quiet entertainment.

We may regret the loss of the dense green cover on the trees and the re-emergence of the bare and skeletal branches, yet each tree is casting off those chemicals which it doesn't want, and it is these in the falling leaves which gives them their vivid yellows, reds, russets and golds. When they have fallen to earth to rot down they will renew the cycle of leaf mould, upon which all kinds of things depend: small fungi, insects, larvae, ants and beetles, and in turn new generations of trees, whose seeds are gently wrapped in a quilt of warm, damp, decaying leaves. This will give them an opportunity to grow again, perhaps in the lighter spaces left by the trees cast down by the great gales in recent years. Other woodland plants will find a foothold in these newly created glades, and gain protection among the broken branches or horizontal tree trunks. So will small animals and birds find refuges in holes and under bark, and in the tunnels shattered branches have made.

We conceive of death as final, yet to all other living systems it is a mere pause on an eternal cycle. The fallen leaves are reprocessed and become growth for next year's leaves. Bodies of animals make food, their bones decay and nourish the soil, nothing is lost, it is all returned and turned again into new life. We have grown up in traditions where death leads only to a change of state, an entry into purgatory or a heaven world, whereas in other lands, in other cultures, a human death is only a momentary pause in the on-going chain of incarnations, a time for rest and reflection. There is a famous Eastern saying 'I died as a stone and was reborn as a plant. I died as a plant and I was reborn as an animal. I died as an animal and was reborn as a human being. When has my death ever led to my being diminished?'

To those with open eyes and a feeling for Nature, it is easy to see this sombre and perhaps dripping month as one of plenty, of stocking up before withdrawing into a necessary seasonal rest. We become frantic, seeking more heat than we need, acquiring stores of things and clothes against the winter, squandering resources, and living in fear of what might happen. We need to relearn how to deal with Autumn. To see it as a time of celebration of life, of summing up, rewarding ourselves for the achievements we have gained, or for having the strength to accept failure. It is the mistakes in life which teach us valuable lessons. Sometimes we have to try and accept that we have reached too far, or shot too high, yet we still have the ability and adaptability to change, and grow. So does nature. A plant may reach out an unthinking tendril and grab another stem only to be snapped off in a gust of wind. It then reaches out again, perhaps in a different direction. The plant is not harmed. We are seldom harmed by failure, even if our pride is bruised or our egos shocked.

In the woodlands and glens of Scotland the stags are rutting, battling for harems of does and hinds, and settling territorial disputes, not for their own sake, but for that of their children. They want the best feeding area, the most wives, the most sheltered wintering place, and it is the stag with the most strength and determination who sires the most fawns for the following year. When two stags battle they are doing so as a test of strength and courage rather than as an attempt to kill each other. Most animals fight for mating rights, for territory or to defend their family from harm, and once the weaker opponent has been chased a sufficient distance he is left alone. The

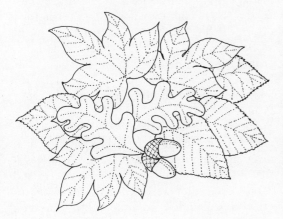

special places chosen by animals have detectable energies, as has been shown by experiments carried out by dowsers. These sensers of underground water, hidden minerals and lost items can also detect, with their hands, or a dowsing rod, areas with increased 'Earth Energy', and it is these places that the stags fight over. Watch any cat, dog or cow choosing a place to rest and you will see that they circle about until they feel comfortable; dowsers do much the same.

Cider Making

October is above anything else the cider making month. The apples are beaten from the trees into blankets, in the old ways, and even fallen and partly rotten apples are included in the fruit taken to the press. In 1657 it was recorded 'The old sorts of apple are the most valuable for cider, such as Stire, Golden-pippin, Hagloe crab, Harveys, Bradys, Red-streak, Woodcock, Moyle, Gennetmoyle, red and yellow Musks, Fox-whelp, Loan, Old Pearmains, Dymock-red and Ten Commandments', among others. A wonderful list. These or whatever was to hand were gathered, or brought down from the trees on to straw and taken into shelter, where they were spread out to 'sweat' for a while. The rotten apples are supposed to clear the finished cider, and are very juicy.

Old cider presses are still to be seen outside country pubs, and inside some of the more enterprising ones, whose owners, seeing a place in the market for home-made, organic or naturally fermented cider, fresh-pressed apple juice, cidervinegar and anything else, like 'perry' which is pear cider, have restored them and put them to use. The apples are crushed, usually with a millstone on edge, turned by hefty people, a horse or, I suppose these days, a motor. The crushed pulp and juice is layered into the cider press between sacking in what are called 'cheeses'. Sometimes straw is included to filter the pulp, and the great plates of the press are screwed together so that all the juice which can be squeezed from the cheese is brought out. This is run into fermenting casks to work until approved by the maker. Really rough cider or scrumpy, as it is called in some places, is an acquired taste, and some of the Somerset pubs who sell their own brew won't sell it to tourists or during the peak holiday season, for they are well aware of how potent this strongly flavoured apple drink can be.

meadows, the gates to the sluices were inspected to be ready to close when the first frosts were felt, often at the end of October, so that water could cover the precious grasslands to give early feed in the spring.

Preparing for Winter

Making drinks, cordials and beer was an ordinary part of every farm wife's duty, but at this season of fruity riches she would be especially busy. Having observed the departure of the swallows, and seeing the nights drawing in, she would prepare the crocks to make tasty and curative cordials, liniments for man and animals, and many kinds of pastes and potions to cleanse the skin, heal cuts and bruises or knit sprains or broken bones. The last of the green herbs would have been hung in the rafters to dry for culinary and other purposes and it was a time for asking a blessing upon the work, that all which was stored would remain fit to eat and not go mouldy or sour. Elderberries would be gathered to make wine or a thicker syrupy cordial for chest complaints, sloes would be made into a draught against stomach cramps and diarrhoea. Lavender and Lad's Love would be laid among stored linens and clothes to sweeten them and deter insects. Corn dollies in the local pattern would have been woven and placed above the hearth as a constant reminder of spring and sowing that was to come, and to keep the spirit of the corn alive and warm in the winter.

Out of doors it was a time of gathering in the last of the vegetables to be stored, collecting nuts, and picking mushrooms to dry for winter use. Animals would begin to be rounded up and the horn calls across the hills as various stockmen and shepherds worked their ways across unfenced moorland or the edges of forest to collect their straying beasts were heard from dawn to dusk. Hurdles would be brought out to pen groups of beasts, and sheep and rams would be inspected for disease, foot rot or any other ill, before being set to mate to produce early lambs. Hedges and ditches would be gone over so that winter winds and rains would not destroy them, and flood water could run off the fields. If there were water

October Folk Customs

Although this is not generally a time for dances it has produced many folk customs, carried out during October and early November, which are concerned with prediction and prognostication. Most people are aware of the festival of Hallowe'en at the end of October, but there are a number of less widely known minor folk traditions which follow similar lines. Writers in the early eighteenth century observed that it was customary to inspect oak-apples, around the beginning of October, which if found to contain spiders warned of a hard winter and a difficult year ahead; if they had flies inside it meant good luck and plenty. If the oak-apples were empty, a dearth would follow. The dryness or wetness within betokened the weather for the coming year.

Another custom for young ladies, who, it would seem, found numerous ways of trying to detect who their future husbands might be, took place on St Faith's Day, 6 October. They would bake a special cake, turn it nine times (nine being a number associated with the Moon and with divination in general) cut it into twenty-seven tiny slivers and pass these through a long-married lady's wedding ring. They would then pray to St Faith, a virgin martyr, for a vision of their husband to be, whom they hoped to meet in their dreams. If St Faith had no husband one might wonder how she could help other young ladies change their marital state!

Nuts, conkers, apple pips, apple peel, mirrors and candles were all brought into use to detect future husbands, or to find solutions to other problems. Sometimes cob nuts or chestnuts were paired and named after the girl and her potential lover and both thrown into the fire. If they sizzled into ash quietly together then a long and happy association was predicted, but if one or other burst and flew from the hearth it meant a stormy and brief encounter. An apple might be

apple peel, and in due course married a man called George, or that you dreamed of nets, and your future husband brought you net stockings, or was a fisherman, or worked in a circus as a high wire dancer above a safety net! The spell worked, and the prediction came true. You may have helped it along by rejecting Bill, or turning down a brush salesman who had no nets in his suitcase, but that also is the nature of prediction and choice. A self-fulfilled prediction is just as true as one in which only Fate took a hand.

The Season of Hallowe'en

Hallowe'en was originally a season, not a single night; it was celebrated over the last couple of weeks in October. It used to be a time of family reunions, for when many people worked away from home in residential jobs or factories, and before there were reliable transport systems, it was necessary to visit parents to be given winter clothing or exchange gifts before travel became impossible for months at a time. It was also a time when those who cared for livestock roaming at large came home to greet those whom they had not seen for some time, meet new babies born in the summer, and learn of those who had passed away during their absences. Longer ago it was a time when the Lord of a Manor or Castle would gather together all his retinue – servants, tenants, serfs, soldiers and the craftspeople who worked for him – to see who was under his control. He would be expected to give a feast and probably dismiss the soldiery to their homes, now that the fighting season, limited by inclement weather, was over.

As at Beltane, the other great Fire Festival of the pagan Celts, Hallowe'en was an occasion when bonfires were lit to guide people home, or welcome travellers to the hall. Again there would be spells of protection on all who were to winter together, to prevent food spoiling or being eaten by rats, to prevent quarrels spreading through a tightly-knit community and flaring into open conflict, and to name and bless children, or unions of people. The Celtic name of this season, which fell probably at the full moon following the first real frost in the area, was Samhain, or

carefully peeled in a magical spiral and the entire strip cast over the left shoulder, carefully avoiding the demon, which popular folklore insisted lurked there. It would fall on the floor in the shape of an initial letter of a future or enduring love.

Somehow it had remained in the Collective Unconscious of people that the end of October betokened a time when there might be a rift in the laws of Nature, which permitted the intrusion of knowledge about the past and future to be combined. Dreams around this time of year were looked upon as possible omens of things to come. Traditions like this do not succeed or continue to be practised unless there is a fair chance that they produce results. This is the underlying principle of many folk customs. If you ask a blessing in a particular way, on a special day, making ritual gestures, offerings of flowers, dances, songs, garlands or rags, and the result which you have asked for comes into being, then that spell, prayer or invocation has worked. You are never in a position to experience what might have happened if you had not performed the traditional act. Most magical charms and spells work like that. You follow the rules and what you wanted, more or less, happens. If you had not done the ritual or made the offering who knows what might have come to pass. What you do know, however, and hold as evidence as to the success of the procedure, is that you did indeed see the letter 'G' in

Summer's End. It is the closing of the door to the year opened at Beltane or May Day, and a gathering in and counting of all that was to be known.

Just as at the beginning of May there are customs to do with common rights, at the end of October there are certain traditions governing the gathering of wood or turf or peat for the fire, and the rights to pasture pigs in this nutting season where they can fatten up on beechmast, acorns, roots and fallen fruit. One of these is the right of Foresters around Epping to cut dead wood for the hearth. This right was an annoyance to certain landowners and one year they planned to prevent the ritual from which the rights derived from taking place. The woodcutters had to cut with axes enough wood to make a bonfire on the due date, but the landlords' men waylaid the party and locked them in a barn. Fortunately, the landlords' men, in their haste to complete the deed, forgot to take away the axes from the foresters. These men chopped their way out of the barn doors, cut their tree, made the bonfire and so hold their rights to this day!

Other autumnal customs include the tradition of tolling 'Lost in the Dark Bells' to guide travellers on unlit roads and through heavily wooded areas to the nearest refuge. There are many medieval tales, from Hampshire to Scotland, of weary and benighted folk being about to fall into bogs, over cliffs or being led astray by Puck or Fairies, but at the critical moment a local church bell was rung, and they were saved. Stories about Curfew or Dead Bells are still told from Newark, from Lincolnshire, Charlton-on-Otmoor in Oxfordshire; Cliffe, Kent, Twyford and Kidderminster, and funds were originally bequeathed by grateful wanderers whose journey was successfully concluded due to these cheering bells. A variety of bells are still rung, either singly at a specific time each night, or in peals on Fair Days or on other local feast dates, probably to call home the lost, but also to ring out the protective magic at this particularly ghostly time of year.

Hallowe'en Night

Hallowe'en Night or All Souls' Eve falls on 31 October. In earlier times this day would almost certainly have been the night of the full moon after the first proper frost. It is thought of as a time of 'ghoulies and ghosties and long-leggedy beasties and things that go bump in the night', a time when time stands still and beings from the Other Side, spirits of the recently dead and long-

dead ancestors walk abroad. In many places a great bonfire is lit at sunset, if there is one on this chilly eve, a special feast is prepared, and a place left empty for the unseen visitor. In some pagan traditions this place is set for the Great Mother, the original ancestor of the family or clan, from whom all are descended, and who is especially welcomed on this date, to bring blessing, hear news, and confer about the future through various kinds of divination. Although it is a time for remembering the dead, a tradition which fills the end of October and the first couple of weeks in November, it is also a time for looking forward to the birth of babies. According to one old tradition, not only do the spirits of the dead appear in the bonfire smoke, but the candles call in the souls of children who are to be born in the coming year, to meet their parents and inspect their future home.

Many of the aspects of Hallowe'en parties and the special games played only then have extremely ancient roots. To most of the Celtic people, apples were symbols of immortality. If you cut one crossways you will find the place where the seeds are forms a perfect five-pointed star or pentagram, an ancient symbol of magic and protection. A star is also a symbol of guidance or hope for a better future. 'Bobbing for Apples' in a bowl or bucket of water or 'Snapping at Apples' tied by their stalks to an overhead beam on a long string, so that in both cases the daring or determined can catch one in their teeth, is actually a lottery about eternal life. Win an apple and gain the prize of good luck or health for the coming year; miss and get half-drowned or a bonk on the nose from a flying fruit!

Other prediction games include pricking an egg so that the white oozes through the small hole to fall into hot water where it cooks into strange shapes, supposed to be indications of a new lover or event to come. In Cornwall lead, no doubt filched from a church roof, to make it magical, was melted, and this was carefully poured into water and again the cooled lump examined in the way a Roman haruspex would pore over the entrails of a stricken hen. Sometimes it was candle wax dripped into a divinatory bowl which was examined closely for hints of what sort of person might fulfil a wish. Looking at your face

in a mirror at midnight by the light of a candle was another way of attracting the shade or double of your intended, so that his or her face might appear next to yours in the glass. All kinds of spells and incantations were said in order to scare the looker into the right, receptive frame of mind for a blowing curtain or wisp of smoke half-seen from the corner of the eye to turn into a face.

There are lots of children's customs attached to this time of year, and though some people consider that 'Trick or Treat' has been imported from America, it was here first. There are three different elements which are combined in different ways; one is the making of Punkies (pumpkin or turnip or swede lanterns); another is the dressing up in all sorts of ghostly or bewitching costumes; and the third is knocking on neighbour's doors, demanding sweets or offering to do mischief. The pumpkin, which originates from America, is a newer and easier vegetable from which to carve staring faces with jagged teeth, and glaring eyes which glow with the light of a candle end set within. These used to be set about on gateposts, or in trees, to scare away evil spirits. In some places there are competitions to see who can carve the most fiendish-looking faces, or the most amusing.

Dressing up, blacking the face with soot, wearing clothes too big, or inside-out or back-to-front, decking yourself with rags, ribbons or even newspaper strips have been associated with many festivals where there is a worry about Unseen Forces. It has always been thought that the devil, or harmful sprites or, where they are still feared, the fairies, are bemused by such changed attire. Any kind of disguise would be enough to stop anything nasty following you home, if you had been away for a while. Costumes which seem to be preferred these days for the Hallowe'en Parties which are becoming popular are those of witches, vampires, ghosts, wizards or assorted, green-faced demons. Wearing masks and playing scary games is also part of the increasingly widespread habit.

Some people are afraid that allowing youngsters to take part in the Punkie Night celebrations, or attend a Hallowe'en Party, will encourage them to do unpleasant things to people who annoy them. This was one of the roots of the old festival, especially where you disguised yourself and turned up on a disliked neighbour's doorstep, threatening to perform some small act of vandalism, or anything with a high nuisance value, unless he repaid a debt, or stopped something which annoyed you. He could bribe you to go away with some small gift, or he could slam the door in your face, and expect the minor retribution which you had suggested would take place. Removing gates was always part of this tradition, or whitewash over house windows, hiding horses or cows, or chaining up all the house doors so no one could get out. It was a day on which vengeance could be exacted, but there were always unwritten rules that no one would be harmed, nor animals upset or damaged.

The idea of ghosts was old long before Christianity came to these shores, and this ancient Feast of ending one year and beginning a new year was a natural time when beings from all levels of existence should get together. It was a time of paying debts, settling quarrels and renewing all the personal, unwritten contracts by which ancient society was bound together. The games children play allow them to come to terms with scary ideas in a gentle and fun-filled way. They can learn to understand their fears of the dark, of death and of strange happenings in an unthreatening way, so that if something really frightening should happen to them they have a way of explaining it to adults, and be understood. Children know the difference between 'pretend' and 'real'; they are also far more aware of ghosts and have psychic experiences for which even the language of well-informed adults is often inadequate, so they cannot always explain what they have seen or heard. When they try to tell us it is usually put down to over-active imaginations, and rather than being used as an opportunity to communicate, it is often ignored.

Life in Death

Life does have more dimensions than most people are aware of in their everyday lives, there are strange and unexplained things going on around us all the while, but it is easy to dismiss them. Thousands of people have seen ghosts, felt the atmosphere of houses as either cold and stark or welcoming and friendly. They seldom complain about the latter experience. Many people have predictive dreams, don't get on planes which crash, avoid other disasters because of hunches. It is seasonal festivals like Hallowe'en which allow some of these darker, repressed ideas to come to the surface in a light and playful way, and this time should be celebrated as a release. It is useful to have a day or two to remember the lives and loving of those of our friends and family who have died. It isn't morbid to think about a beloved Aunt or Grandpa who is not there to share the fun, to recall the good times that were shared, the tears and the laughter. That is a healing thing, and many old customs celebrate the life of the deceased, rather than being regretful and guilt-ridden after his death. Hallowe'en is a good time to share with those close to you the words which express your love and caring. Those are nearly always the ones which you most regret never having said while your dear one was alive. Find a moment, make them laugh and then say 'I love you!'

Real witches, of whom there are an increasing and beneficial number these days (for they are taking back the roles of folk healer, diviner, or wart charmer) celebrate Samhain or Hallowe'en as the Feast of Life in Death. There is a coming together of the whole family, clan or coven so that ideas may be exchanged. The Earth Mother and the Sky or Harvest Lord are called upon to bless the people, and part of their cyclic life story is enacted. The Sun God is descending into the Otherworld to look after the spirits of the dead and the unborn, granting them rest and renewal. The Goddess is seen as the Wise Old Woman, the caring, but sometimes crotchety old Grandmother, who brings gifts but may also scold. She is also sinking into the Otherworld as all Nature withdraws for its winter rest, and in the darkness under the Earth she will be renewed, to return as Mother at Yule, and as the Maiden in the first days of Spring. The new pagans, of many traditions, both old and reinvented, do care for the Earth, her sacred places and her turning cycles.

LIBRA, THE SCALES

Those whose birthdays fall between about 21 September, the Autumn Equinox and 21 October come into the sign of Libra, the Scales. This is an air sign, ruled by the planet Venus, so those born then will share the love of beauty and a love of justice. Their main objective in life is a combination of peace and harmony. They are law abiding, but can be very determined if they feel their sense of fair play has been exceeded. Any kind of quarrel or dispute upsets them, and they are quite likely to vary their own approach in order to avoid a confrontation. They like to be surrounded by beautiful and interesting things, and are often collectors of antiques or works of art. Some are inventors like Robert Stephenson or Michael Faraday, architect Sir Christopher Wren, philosopher Friedrich Nietzsche, psychiatrist R.D. Laing or magical experimenter with a worse than deserved reputation, Aleister Crowley.

Librans, because of their flair for making their surroundings look and feel attractive, can be suited by many colours, especially greens and blues, and some of the more smokey or rose pinks, dull gold or deep violet. Librans are linked with the planet Venus, which is symbolised by the metal copper; copper might be used to decorate their homes, or made into jewellery, together with large semi-precious stones such as rose quartz, aventurine, malachite, jade, emeralds, and tourmalines, perhaps in chunky settings, or used in modern ways.

As Libra folk are interested in truth and justice they make good Astrologers. Everyone's horoscope is as individual as their fingerprints, because within each chart there are the positions and interrelationships of twelve houses, or signs of the zodiac, and the ten wandering stars or planets whose influences incline each of us towards energy or peace, intellectual pursuits or love of music. From very ancient times the sky was divided into twelve parts, roughly covered by the constellations or inter-linked patterns of stars which we know as the signs of the zodiac. It is the sun, on the day of our birth, as it rises against these sets of stars, which gives us our sun sign or sign of the zodiac. The Moon, Mars, Mercury, Jupiter, Venus, Saturn, Pluto, Neptune, and Uranus each occupy an original position in our charts, depending on the exact moment of birth, over the place where we were born. A good astrologer will set up the chart marking the positions of these planets within the houses, and other things which influence us, like the Mid-heaven point, and the North and South Nodes of the Moon. It is the combination of all these influences which give us the strengths and weaknesses of character and health, our direction in life, love and interests, as well as being markers towards a successful career. To interpret the exact interactions of all these powers requires training, time and a great sense of responsibility. A well prepared horoscope explained by an experienced astrologer can be a great help, in whichever sign your birthday falls.

Because Librans are agreeable, sociable and relaxed people who like to earn approval from people they deal with, the one-to-one work of astrologers, or of solicitors, artists, or social workers often appeals to them. Their sense of natural justice and fair play ensures that they are well respected.

October Recipes

Hallowe'en Parties

Hallowe'en parties provide the opportunity for original cooks to produce some really bizarre dishes, favouring such colours as black, orange and purple. These go down well with children and adults alike.

Eyeball Jelly is very simple, involving dark red jelly (black cherry or blackcurrant flavour) made with a little water into which is stirred a tin of lychees and their juice. The end result is strange white objects in the dark red, which look extremely sinister but taste good.

Worm Soup is another quick favourite made with a large tin, or quantity of homemade, tomato soup, into which is stirred some cooked spaghetti, cut into worm-lengths, or macaroni shapes.

Poison Toadstools can be made from halved hard-boiled eggs topped by halved tomatoes, with spots of mayonnaise added for colour.

Stagnant Ponds can be made by halving some ripe avocados, mixing the mashed flesh with a little onion, finely chopped or blended green pepper, cucumber and tomato, and this mix put back into the avocado shells with the green parts of mustard and cress sprinkled over them.

Red Salads can be made of a mixture of red lettuce leaves, red cabbage, red pepper, black olives, radishes, tomato slices and red apple with the skin left on.

Despite their appearance, all these dishes taste delicious and can form parts of a really weird Hallowe'en Supper, especially if you add in a few games, such as 'Musical Bat': passing a bat, (plastic) or, if preferred, a spider, round until someone stops the music, so that the bat holder leaves the ring. The last survivor keeps the bat. 'Pass the Pumpkin' involves a roughly made parcel with newspaper wrappings, with 'nasty' forfeits between the layers. When the music stops the person holding it unwraps a layer, finds the forfeit and then has to do whatever it says. Or you can get your guests to carve out a turnip (swede, pumpkin or mangelwurzel) into a hideous-faced lantern. Have fun and watch out for the family ghosts!

Colcannon

Serve this warming dish on Hallowe'en night.

2 oz/60g/¼ cup dripping
1 lb/500g/2 cups mashed cooked potatoes
½ lb/250g/2½ cups shredded cabbage
½ lb/250g/2 cups onions (chopped)
½ lb/250g/1 cup bacon (cut into small cubes)
salt and pepper
1 tbsp chopped parsley

Melt the dripping in a large frying pan and add the vegetables. Cook together until browned. Add the bacon and cook that. Season to taste and serve on a large platter with the parsley sprinkled over the top.

Sloe Gin

The sloes should not be picked until after the first frost. Prick the cleaned sloes with a darning needle or a fork and drop them into a bottle or kilner jar until it is one third full. Add 8 oz sugar for each pound of sloes used, and top up with gin until sloes and sugar are completely covered. Shake daily until the sugar has dissolved. Leave for three months, shaking occasionally, then strain and bottle.

Don't throw away the gin-soaked sloes. The fruit can be shopped off and used in fruit puddings, or with melted chocolate to make a delicious sweet.

Carve a Hallow'en Pumpkin Lantern

To make one of these Pumpkin Lanterns you need a decent-sized pumpkin. In Britain, swedes and turnips are traditionally used, but these are much harder to carve.

Slice off the top of the pumpkin or swede, as in the picture, leaving the stem. With a pumpkin, the lid can be cut off as a zigzag shape, if you prefer. Hollow out the vegetable, saving the inside to make pumpkin pie or soup, or mashed swede as a vegetable dish. As pumpkins have quite firm shells these can be scooped out fairly thoroughly. The triangular nose, eyes and sharp teeth in a grin can be carefully cut with a vegetable knife. You can let your imagination have free rein, especially if you are making several lanterns. A nightlight or three in their metal holders can then be placed inside the hollowed out face to shine out in the dark at a Hallowe'en party. Pumpkins are rather heavy so need to sit on a table, but swede, turnip or even sugar beet lanterns can have a loop of coat hanger wire through the top and then be hung on a pole to take 'Trick or Treating'.

Rather than waste the flesh of the pumpkin when you have made your hallowe'en lanterns, it can be used to make a tasty pie or soup.

To make pumpkin soup, cut the pumpkin flesh into cubes and cook in water for about 20 minutes, or until tender. Drain and puree. Melt 1 oz butter in a pan and stir in 1 tbsp flour to make a smooth paste. Slowly stir in 1 pint of milk for each pound of pumpkin used. Add the pumpkin puree and salt, pepper, herbs and sugar to taste. Serve hot.

OCTOBER SONG

Cock Robin

Who killed Cock Robin?
'I,' said the sparrow,
'With my bow and arrow,
I killed Cock Robin.'

Chorus

All the birds of the air
Fell a-sighing and a-sobbing
When they heard of the death
Of poor Cock Robin,
When they heard of the death
Of poor Cock Robin.

Who saw him die?
'I,' said the fly,
'With my little eye,
I saw him die.'

Who'll toll the bell?
'I,' said the bull,
'Because I can pull,
I'll toll the bell.'

Who'll dig his grave?
'I,' said the owl,
'With my little trowel,
I'll dig his grave.

Who'll be his parson?
'I,' said the rook,
'With my bell and book,
I'll be the parson.'

Who'll be chief mourner?
'I,' said the dove,
'I'll mourn for my love,
I'll be chief mourner.'

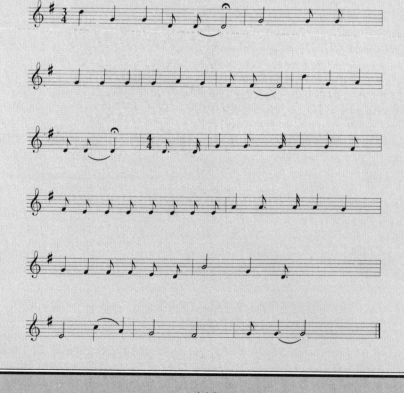

118

NOVEMBER

November comes like a warrior,
With a stain of blood upon his brazen mail.
His crimson scarf is rent.
His scarlet banner drips with gore.
His step is like a flail upon the threshing floor.

Longfellow: *'Autumn'*

All Soul's Day

November begins where October left off, still in a state of death-in-life, and this theme recurs in a variety of ways during the month. When the Christian church tried to overcome the earlier pagan ideas about Hallowe'en being a time of ghosts and ancestor remembrance, they made 1 November All Soul's Day, a time when it was Christianly right and proper to remember those who had gone before. It was also All Saint's Day so that not only the ordinary mortal dead could be called to mind, but also all those myriad saints (some real, some imaginary; some folk memories of guardian spirits or fairy women) who might be overlooked in the sanctified calendar. In the Midlands there was a tradition of baking Soul Cakes, or biscuits, and parties of Soulers would go from house to house, singing a song and begging for these cakes in memory of the dead of the community.

In some of these processions there was a horse head or skull upon a staff carried among the Soulers, sometimes called the 'Hooden' or 'Hodening Horse', similar to the Mari Lwyd, which is the White Mare carried in New Year rituals in

Wales. As the beginning of November was the Celtic New Year there may be a direct link. Again we have a rite involving a horse; they turn up at almost all the main seasonal festivals, either as real horses, pulling decorated carts, or in the form of 'gallopers' on old roundabouts at fairs. Some folklorists avow that the Hooden Horse relates to the Norse God, Odin, or Woden, after whom our Wednesday is named. He rode an eight-legged horse called Sleipnir, and became a teacher, having discovered the magical Runes whilst undergoing an ordeal in an ash tree. He was usually accompanied by two ravens, named Thought and Memory. There are only a few Norse connections in the widespread folk festivals of Britain, although the Anglo-Saxons did leave their traces in the names of places.

Bonfire Night

What most people in Britain associate with the beginning of November is Bonfire Night, an opportunity for watching fireworks, being out later than usual on dark evenings and perhaps seeing a procession of torch-lit characters in Fancy Dress, as is the practice in Sussex and other places.

Although Guy Fawkes Night with its tradition of burning a guy or effigy can only date back to the seventeenth century, at this time there was an older fire festival, now known as Hallowe'en. On 5 November, 1605, Guy Fawkes and some of his fellow conspirators were arrested under the Houses of Parliament accompanied by a large quantity of gunpowder with which, it became apparent, they were not making celebratory fireworks. Guy Fawkes was put to death and we have celebrated the saving of Parliament ever since. Once again this has become an opportunity when children with a mercenary bent are out on the steets, often quite early in October, with a stuffed effigy, plaintively begging for 'Pennies for the Guy'. 'Remember, remember the Fifth of November, With gunpowder, treason and plot. I see no reason why gunpowder treason should ever be forgot!'

The money raised by these forays on to street corners by youngsters is supposed to be used to buy fireworks, but as the law gets stricter and it becomes more common for there to be municipal Bonfire Parties, or charity fund-raising events, centred round the kind of firework display that few individuals could afford to put on, then this form of begging must have another use.

As mentioned before, bonfires were an essential part of the Hallowe'en celebrations. Burning effigies or man-shaped green figures goes back before the Roman invasion, especially at this critical time in the year, when the farming harvests had been brought in, and care was needed to ensure that the new growth of life would follow in the spring. All kinds of offerings would have been traditional, although the kinds which tend to have survived are special cakes or sweets, and bunches of flowers, coloured leaves or berries.

Although the Bonfire Party is a common event, and today's part-firework celebrations and part-barbecues have little enough to do with the blowing up of Parliament, the whole concept of having some sort of bright entertainment to look forward to at this misty and gloomy time of year is an excellent one. In Lewes, where seventeen Protestant Martyrs were burned at the stake during the religious to-ing and fro-ing, the whole Bonfire idea has been brought to a fine art, and occupies not only the night of 5 November itself, but many Saturday nights before and sometimes after this date. Every village in that part of Sussex, and some in Kent, has its own Bonfire Society, Lewes having several different ones. Each has its own 'uniform' of outlandish or historical costume, and during flaming torch-lit processions down the streets of each place in turn, these gaily dressed characters collect for local charities from the huge lines of people who come to see the whole show: the procession, the bonfires, and the firework displays.

In Lewes itself, there is not merely a Guy, but a huge inflammable effigy of some current set of enemies which rides on the back of a truck through the narrow, hilly and twisting streets to the place of its immolation later at night. Parties of Vikings, of Zulus complete with bones through their noses and huge headdresses of ostrich feathers, mock leopardskin and all manner of shiny trappings, or Pirates with their own Society banner carried aloft, march through the streets. There are Cowboys and Indians, Siamese Dancers in spangled costumes, King Henry VIII and his six wives, Milkmaids and Shepherds from one of the local villages; exotic and less dramatic, all process to the hill-top bonfires.

Another part of this exciting celebration is the burning of the effigy of the Pope, Paul IV, the one who was responsible for the roasting of the local Protestants so long ago. The cries with which his fiery end is met makes one aware of what it must have felt like to be at a public execution. The air is electric with screams of 'Burn the Pope', often with strongly Irish accents! It is a fearful moment and the emotion and feelings caused by this archaic practice is something to experience.

> Guy, guy, guy, hang him up high,
> Put him on a bonfire and there let him die.

sung to a plaintive tune in a minor key was once one of the traditional songs at this time, along with the more familiar one! 'Remember, remember the Fifth of November' or the street children's chant:

Penny for the guy, penny for the guy,
If you haven't got a penny a ha'penny will do,
If you haven't got a ha'penny, then God Bless you!

Burning Barrels and Boats

Not only are flaming torches carried through the streets, but a burning barrel, perhaps yet another mystic signal to the declining sun, found in many of the winter celebrations, is carried through the streets of Lewes, to be cast over the bridge into the River Adur. In other towns there used to be a kind of relay race with a barrel of burning tar, being carried along a predetermined route by teams of men whose heads and faces were protected by little more than soaking wet sacking. The civil authorities in Whitney, Oxfordshire, seem to have brought this fiery and riotous custom to an end, but in Ottery St Mary, Devon, tar barrels are still carried through the streets at night by the men, and during the afternoon by boys. These were perhaps tests of strength and endurance, as well as being a kind of flaming reminder for the need for heat from the sun.

In Rye, in Sussex, a week or so after 5 November, they have their own Bonfire Processions, and this time the centrepiece is a small boat or ship. Rye was once on the coast, and still has many yachts and boats moored in its winding river. It has steep cliffs which once had the seas at their feet, but now have level fields from which the water has withdrawn. To commemorate the fishing and boating activities, a model of a galleon, or a real, wrecked boat, is used as the focus of the activities. Processions of the Lewes Bonfire Boys in their colourful costumes, and groups from other local towns and villages, all make their way through the steep, cobbled streets.

There are also illuminated floats from businesses, or Girl Guides and Young Farmers' Clubs, showing what a bit of imagination and ingenuity can produce. Getting larger vehicles through the narrow lanes of Rye is a penance in itself. Gradually the whole gathering makes its way to the lower fields where the bonfire and its sacrificial ship are waiting, and the local dignitary sets fire to the pile. Fireworks explode in the dark sky above the bonfire, set off from a safe distance, and the flares are answered from above on the cliff where individuals or rival parties set off rockets, flares and screaming dragon fireworks.

Eventually the flames reach the rigging of the ship, flare across the spread sails and engulf the shape in a roar of scarlet and gold. Sparks streak up into the darkness. All around, illuminated in the flame light, are the Pirates, Cavaliers, Zulus, Dancing Girls, St Trinian's Scholars, the Cowboys, Vikings and many more, as well as folk from both nearby and far away. All come to munch hot dogs from the vans and yell with delight as especially wonderful fire drakes swoosh across the sky, or explode like the birth of the Universe in a million silver stars. Children hug their parents or ride on shoulders, fascinated and frightened at the same time by the wildly leaping flames, so uncommon in centrally heated houses now. They wince at the bangs, or scream for louder noises, and when unattended rush towards the towering inferno to marvel at the heat and light there.

The Devil's Stone

November 5 has other celebrations, and one at Shebbear seems to retain some aspects of an ancient ritual. Shebbear is a small village under the skirts of the North Devon hills, at the centre of a triangle between Holsworthy, Great Torrington and Okehampton. Outside its church there is a large red stone boulder, perhaps abandoned in the Ice Age. This is the Devil's Stone, and is supposed to be the lid of Hell. There are lots of Devil's stones and rockpiles and uncompleted building projects linked with diabolical intervention, scattered about the British Isles. There are many traditions which tell how the Devil, having nothing better to do, decided to interfere in the building of churches, bridges, castles and other major constructions. Arriving invisible and undetected at night he threw down the foundations, or carried them off in his apron to some preferred site. From the days before King Arthur, when the Saxon Vortigern was having trouble setting up a castle because it kept being demonically demolished (until the young Merlin was invited to explain the phenomenon) to more recent Christian churches with problems, it is the Devil who is supposed to be involved. Often the underlying cause might have been local earth tremors, or unstable rock, but folklore demands a more dramatic solution to these little dilemmas.

Anyway, on 5 November, to the sound of the church's peal of six bells, some sturdy local folk, with long bars and a few pints of ale from the Devil's Stone public house, set about turning over this particular rock. It is said that unless this custom is carried out each year the land will fail, and all sorts of dreadful things befall. Perhaps these days it wards off motorways or country hotels in this beautiful and unspoiled area of Devon. Beneath the oak tree where it has rested for millennia, the Devil's Stone is lifted, heaved, and laid to rest the other way up for another year. Perhaps all the other diabolical rock works also shift in their beds at this season when the veils between the here-and-now and the hereafter are thin, and waver in the November nights.

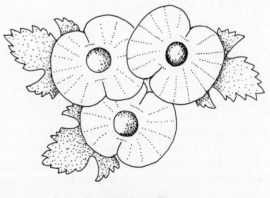

Armistice Day

Recollection and Remembrance are always in people's mind at this dark season, and it is on 11 November that many people recall the ones they loved and lost in war, and deck the war memorial on many a city square or village green with new wreaths of artificial red poppies, recalling the ones that once bloomed in shattered Flanders Fields. On this eleventh day of the eleventh month, on the eleventh hour the Armistice brought the end to the First World War, the war to end war.

November 11 is also Martinmas, honouring the soldier saint who cut his scarlet cloak in half to give part to a beggar. November was always a time of blood-letting, when the use of leeches was a popular treatment for many ills. The sacrificed dead of two World Wars, conflicts in Northern Ireland and the killing and maiming of helpless civilians of all religious persuasions, the Gulf Conflict, battles over land, oil, drugs, human rights and human wrongs must have let more than enough blood for the most cruel of gods to be satisfied.

Now, on the Sunday which follows 11 November there is a great solemn procession to the Cenotaph, the Nation's mourning monument, with military bands playing sombre music in slow time, and all the leaders, political, royal and from the armed services paying homage to those who gave their lives in wars. Two generations have now grown up since the last great conflict, and the buying and wearing of the artificial poppies sold in aid of those crippled in battle is becoming less well understood. Slowly the black-clad contingent from the Royal Family comes forward to lay their wreaths of silken poppies, and the politicians from all parties and the various military, naval and airforce representatives in turn make this useless gesture. How can the fading fake flowers aid the spirits of those who were blown up, shot, drowned, starved, buried, beaten or maimed, unless those in power who lay the tributes make certain there will be no further conflicts, no more useless spilling of blood?

When the poignant sounds of the 'Last Post' echo across the hushed pavements of Whitehall, and the silent tears run unheeded down wrinkled cheeks, and the fresh-eyed faces of young soldiers, airmen, marines and sailors all seem to hope that their turn at real conflict will never come, there is a moment of awe, of recollection and of sorrow, tangible even if viewed on the glowing television screen from a distant, untroubled place. In silence there has to be a moment of grief, of guilt and a feeling of loss for those who have gone before, in peace or war. But this modern version of the older celebration of the life of those who have passed on leaves only yearning and the bitter taste of salty tears. There is no consolation, no end to grief or promise of a light renewed.

Warriors in other times and other lands, facing visible opponents from a sword's length away, would have prepared themselves for battle, putting their life in order. They would go forth saying 'This is a good day to die, my life is complete.' If they survived they would live on renewing that vow. Now our servicemen and women are wiped out by the explosion of shells or bombs fired from miles away or caught unready as civilians at home. No one prepares modern people for death in any circumstances – it is hushed up, talked of in whispers, held at arm's length, and when Death with his sharp scythe enters our houses, we are fearful, and unable to cope. We need to relearn he is a gentle visitor, often bringing a release and peace after pain. We need to learn to celebrate the life of the one who has left us, his achievements, his joys, the laughter or good times that were shared, not eat only the bitter fruit of grief, with tears unshed in conformity with a false tradition.

Thanksgiving Day, USA

Remembrance of a more joyful nature is celebrated in America on the fourth Tuesday of November, Thanksgiving Day. In September 1620, a group of seventy-four men and twenty-eight women sailed from Plymouth in the *Mayflower* to settle in America, where they hoped to find peace and freedom to live and worship as they wished. They are remembered as the 'Pilgrim Fathers'. They landed in Cape Cod Bay, Massachusetts, and called their first settlement Plymouth after the port from which they had sailed. In the Spring of 1621 they planted their first crops. The native people showed them how to grow sweetcorn, sweet potatoes, pumpkins and cranberries, and how to catch and

remembrance and hope for a new future. The bright colours are gone from the flowerbed and the hedgerow, although, all winter long, the red berries of the guelder rose, the rose hips, the hawthorn haws, and the sour fruits of sloe and nightshade might endure until hungry wildlife has need of them. The white tufted old man's beard clambers over the barren thickets, the spikey umbels, empty of seeds of hemlock or hedge parsley, rattle in the winds. In the damp or sheltered places the last fungi moulder, nibbled by ants and mice, and their strange scent lingers in the air.

November was a busy time in the rural household for it was then that the pigs, cattle and other store animals were slaughtered and the meat prepared to last through the winter. There would be immediate feasting on offal and bits and pieces which had to be consumed before they went bad. Usually the sign for setting about these gory but necessary tasks was the first hard frost. Then a carcass could be hung outside or in a barn overnight, before being cut into portions to be smoked, salted or pickled in brine. Everyone would be involved in rendering fat (which was used both in cooking and in simple households as lamp oil), in scraping hides and skins for further use, and in rubbing coarse salt into hams or bacon before it could be smoked. Sausages would be made as well as brawns or 'head cheese', trotters or calves feet would be boiled to give a useful jelly, and the intestines would be cleaned to be used as casings for 'haggis' or sausages. Like the corn and crop harvests, it was a time of frantic work which was vital to the survival of the people during the cruel and barren days of winter. Today we have supermarkets and deep freezes, yet somewhere real people have to deal with the meat, fruit and vegetables to make our lives more enjoyable. These still come from the soil, from farms, and from orchards.

breed wild turkeys. By the autumn of that year they were able to gather their first harvest. Their festivities began on a Thursday in November, when their leader, the governor of Massachusetts Bay, gratefully invited the Indians to join a three day festival to celebrate the harvest and the first year in their new home.

Ever since then Americans, particularly in New England, have celebrated this festival. President Lincoln proclaimed Thanksgiving a national holiday in 1863. There are church services and Thanksgiving dinners of roast turkey with cranberry sauce, candied sweet potatoes and pumpkin pie. It is often a family reunion, and houses are decorated with the flowers and fruits of autumn.

Winter Arrives

Now appear the first signs of winter. Trees are stripped bare of leaves to show their secret and beautiful tracery of branches revealed against a stormy sky. The fading greens on the meadows give way to the taupes and duns of winter, and the darker areas of newly ploughed land make chessboard patterns on the open fields. It is a time of transformation, of opening up and revealing things that the summer garment of leafage has kept hidden. It is a time for revealing your own feelings, perhaps, about death, change,

The Lord Mayor's Show

A different urban symbol of plenty and overflowing material wealth seen at this time of year, in London, is the Lord Mayor's Show. When the new Lord Mayor of London is appointed, he or she rides through the streets of London in the Lord Mayor's Coach to be fêted by all the Livery Companies, and all the representatives of the untold riches of the City. Decorated floats, military and civilian bands, representatives of Merchant Banks, Oil Companies, the Stock Exchange and all those sources of money and invisible earnings parade through the streets to demonstrate the power and influence the City and its workers has on the whole world. It doesn't have the carnival atmosphere that some of the out-of-town processions have, but it is splendid pageantry.

The Lord Mayor's Coach is over two hundred years old, weighs over four tons, and as well as an elaborately carved and gilded exterior is lined with scarlet silk. It is drawn by a team of six grey shire horses and there are bewigged coachmen and liveried attendants on and around it. The modern Lord Mayors must be extremely glad that the journey is over paved roads, for the coach is unsprung and ponderous. It is also a wonderful sight, if the autumn weather is clement and the November sun shines on all its painted splendour. There are many other open coaches and carriages in the procession, as well as a vast array of expensively designed motorised floats and exhibits. In all, the parade stretches over a mile each year, and apart from displaying the wealth and image of the various companies represented, it is an opportunity for the Liveried Companies to ride through the City. There are the Vintners, the Glovers, the Luthiers, the Dyers and representatives of many of the eighty or so Liveried Companies and members of Guilds.

London is the site of many such processions of power and music during the year, and though many parades have an underlying reason, for example the Queen's Official Birthday in June, it is the tradition of ceremony for its own sake which is really being demonstrated. It is hard not to be impressed by the playing and marching of both military and civilian bands, the displays of charitable concerns or the various organisations of young people, smartly turned out in their uniforms, as Sea Cadets, Boys' and Girls' Brigade Members or members of the St John's Ambulance Brigade. It is splendid to watch the fluttering flags, and the great horses of the Household Cavalry or their bands, with the magnificent piebald drum horses, and shining black cavalry chargers, usually so well behaved and calm amid the shouting and cheering crowds. Originally the 'Trooping of the Colour' was done to show an army the banner under which it was to fight, so that they could recognise it in battle. Today this is a display of music, precision marching and horsemanship, to honour these skills in our modern fighting men and women.

Death and Rebirth

November begins with the brilliant bonfires and fireworks of Guy Fawkes Night and progresses through the processions and memories of the various Remembrance Sunday ceremonies to end rather quietly. This period of introspection and silence is really a very important time in the annual cycles of hectic and not-so-hectic happenings throughout the year.

In ancient times this time of year was symbolic of the time after death and before rebirth, seen clearly in the gentle falling leaves of autumn, which in due course would be replaced by new spring greenery. There had been the death of the Summer, the slaughter of excess livestock and the pouring of blood upon the land. The Harvest Lord was cut off with the corn, stacked in barns and threshed to provide wheat for bread throughout the winter.

Our own lives need to have this period of rest and refreshment, and then the forward-looking hope, reborn at Christmas, when a new cycle would begin. All forms of life are cyclic, and when we become aware of that it can have a profound effect on our philosophy. Death is not the end for the plants; they reseed and grow again, or the flowering bulbs send out green spears and brilliant flowers from the same bulb. The human spirit is the same. It shuffles off one set of exterior growth, rests in another, hidden place, and is reborn into a new incarnation. Like the trees it has a different exterior, but the underlying spirit is the same, growing greater in wisdom, perhaps, but not killed by death, only transformed by the silent seasons in between.

SCORPIO, THE SCORPION

November birthdays are largely ruled by Scorpio, the Scorpion, one of the most dynamic of the signs of the zodiac. Scorpios can be extremely tough and ruthless in seemingly gentle matters like love, as well as in business and commerce. They can be cruel in words and hard dealing in all sorts of areas of life. They are energetic and will survive in extremely unpleasant situations where other folk might give in to the pressure. Their ruling planet is Mars, the soldier of the planets, and this can influence a strongly militaristic view of life, combined with Scorpio's natural determination.

They can be good friends, for they are idealistic at heart, and once they have a project in their sights nothing will prevent them carrying it out. Such a project can often be based on a deep love and feeling for a place, or person, or good cause. Being unconventional in outlook and capable of totally wild or shocking approaches to the kinds of problems that stop ordinary people, Scorpios positively thrive on publicity and being in the limelight for some extraordinary exploit. They are very hardworking, mainly in pursuit of their own pleasure or interests, although they can be deeply religious, mystical and psychic, for they are a Water sign, along with Cancer and Pisces. They tend to be ambitious, tenacious and perverse, yet they are caring people and can act as the champions for lost or green causes.

The Scorpion is a creature with a poisonous sting and one of the attributes of the Scorpio is an awareness of death. They may also have a fascination with hidden things, the occult, and secrecy. They will work very hard to get to the bottom of things, and some of their skills, such as ruthlessness and independence, make them good spies. Like the scorpion, too, they will cling on to things, a tendency shared with that other crustacian of the zodiac, Cancer the Crab. In Scorpio's case, however, it may be things other people consider their own! They are often good looking, sexy and charming; they prefer affairs with passionate partners, but can be jealous or moody if their amour decides to stray.

Famous Scorpios include St Augustine, a typical character who is supposed to have prayed 'O God, give me eternal chastity, but not yet!' Poets William Cowper, and the opium user Samuel Taylor Coleridge (who was inspired to write 'Xanadu' until interrupted from his creative work by a casual visitor) and Franz Liszt were all Scorpios, as were Captain Cook, William Hogarth and Benvenuto Cellini, both artists, and Martin Luther, a great religious leader.

The colours most closely associated with Scorpios tend to be any red stones, including fake jewellery, in brilliant gold settings. They do, however, prefer real rubies, especially large ones, and also carnelians, bloodstones, garnets and jasper. The darker side of their natures will appreciate onyx, beryls, topaz and bright turquoise. The colours that they like to wear can include really vivid red and black, but russet, maroon, deep blue and crimson will be to their taste. Scarlet, vibrant purple and burnt orange might be worn for effect for they all love to make dramatic entries to parties, which they very much enjoy. They are good company, and witty and intelligent guests at such events.

Ten Vegetable Soup

This vegetarian supper dish is thick enough to be a main meal, or it can be blended or thinned with stock to make a lighter soup to fill vacuum flasks, or to be reheated over bonfire or barbecue. It is very simple and requires only that there be at least ten vegetables in it; quantities and types depend on you!

Start off with some vegetable stock, and mixed dried herbs and seasoning to taste. Chop up as many seasonal vegetables as you can: potatoes, onions, carrots, swedes, mushrooms, tomatoes, green and red peppers, courgettes, celery, turnips, cabbage, cauliflower, garlic and beans. Dried lentils or split peas (presoaked) are another good ingredient. If you are short of fresh vegetables, add in some frozen ones. Add the vegetables to the stock and simmer for 20 to 30 minutes; the vegetable chunks should still be intact. The broth may be thickened with a little flour or tomato purée.

Montgomeryshire Pheasant

1 pheasant
2 tbsp butter
1 large onion
1 large carrot
1 large leek
1 turnip
pinch of parsley and thyme
salt and pepper
¼ bottle red wine
4 tbsp flour

Prepare the pheasant. Heat the butter in a heavy pan. Lightly fry the bird until it is browned. Take it out and put it to one side. Peel the vegetables and cut them up into small cubes or slices. Put them in the bottom of the pan and add the seasonings. Place the pheasant on the vegetables, pour over the wine and add water to cover. Place the lid on the pan and simmer slowly for two hours. Thicken the liquid with the flour just before serving.

Parkin

Parkin is a moist, sticky ginger cake, traditionally eaten on Guy Fawkes' Night. It should be made a week earlier, to give it time to mature before using.

6 oz/185g plain flour
10 oz/315g oatmeal
6 oz/185g treacle
5 oz/155g butter
4 oz/125g soft brown sugar
¼ pint/150ml milk
1 egg
3 tsp ground ginger
1 tsp ground cinnamon
1 tsp bicarbonate of soda
1 tsp salt

Mix the dry ingredients together. Warm the treacle, butter, sugar and milk in a saucepan until dissolved. Leave to cool. Beat in the egg, then pour into the dry ingredients and beat well until smooth. Pour the mixture into a greased and lined 7 inch baking tray and bake at 180°C/350°F/Gas Mark 4, for about one hour. Allow to cool in the tin for ten minutes before turning out onto a wire rack. Keep in an airtight tin for at least a week before eating.

Children's Punch

2 pints/1.25 litres/5 cups apple juice
½ pint/30cl/1⅓ cups orange juice
1 pint/60cl/2½ cups water
10 cloves
½ tsp ground cinnamon and/or ginger
Sugar and lemon juice to taste
Apple or orange slices to garnish

Put all the ingredients in a pan and heat through gently. Leave the punch off the heat to brew for at least 10 minutes, strain out the spices, and serve warm.

CREATE A BONFIRE PARTY
TABLE DECORATION

Now that more people go to public bonfire celebrations instead of having their own fireworks and fire in the garden some children may miss out on the excitement of these most ephemeral of entertainments. Others are really frightened by the bangs and flashes, as are family pets. This firework table decoration aims to bring the beauty and brightness of fireworks safely (and silently!) into the home.

Decorative fireworks can be made from cardboard rolls, empty detergent bottles or construction paper, lengths of florists' wire, pieces of Christmas tinsel, shiny paper and lots of imagination! The aim is to make a display of a variety of fireworks which appear to be exploding, with silver and gold flashes, rains of sparks, or glittering tails. Make the cases from cylinders decorated with paint or glued-on paper to look like 'Roman Candles', 'Silver Rain' and so on. Stick small twists of tinsel to lengths of florists' wire and tape the wire to the top of the firework to be the sparks. Some stones or modelling clay inside the cylinders will anchor the display, but the wire is thin enough to move and cause the sparklers to glitter. The rocket, fixed to a stick, should have a tail of tinsel or silver and gold streamers. Small gifts could be hidden in each mock firework; you could run a competition to make the most 'explosive' looking display, with a small prize for the winner.

NOVEMBER SONG

Here we go Round the Mulberry Bush

Here we go round the mulberry bush,
The mulberry bush, the mulberry bush;
Here we go round the mulberry bush
On a cold and frosty morning.

This is the way we clap our hands,
Clap our hands, clap our hands;
This is the way we clap our hands
On a cold and frosty morning.

This is the way we brush our shoes ...

This is the way we wash our face ...

This is the way we clean our teeth ...

This is the way we comb our hair ...

DECEMBER

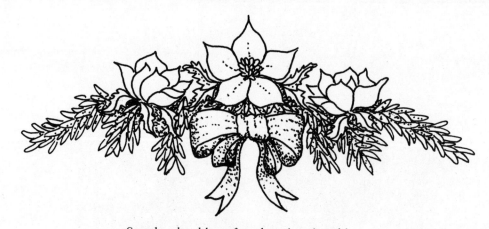

So why should we fear the winter's cold
When under the furrow sleeps the gold?
The earth bears seeds of the future sun
And out of the dark new life will come,
And care with the bells at midnight flees away,
And joy comes in on Christmas morning.

Sylvia Mehta: *'Bells at Midnight'*

The Feast of Christmas

In Christian lands the feast of Christmas must be the best known and most widely celebrated, although it doesn't have the power and mystery of Easter. Sadly, these days it has become largely a commercial time, with cards on sale in August and all the tinsel and fairy lights often appearing before Hallowe'en. In earlier times this was the season of Yuletide, 'Yul' meaning wheel; it was a time of turning and going onwards. There was a lengthy feast in the darkest days, lasting from the Winter Solstice on 21 December until the beginning of January, when it was seen that the Sun was returning because the light was lengthening by a few moments each passing day. We now have a song which recalls the 'Twelve Days of Christmas', on each of which a truelove sent a variety of edible or improbable presents of increasing complexity.

Yuletide was a time of great anxiety to un-tutored and simple folk hundreds of years ago, for they did not have our certainty that the year will revolve and longer days reappear. They had to make all kinds of offerings – fires, decorated trees and supplications – to beg the heat and light of the Sun to return. Many of these very old customs are still with us in our modern festivities, but perhaps we have forgotten, or never knew, from whence they came.

The festival of Advent is celebrated throughout December, and in many places an Advent Crown is made, of tinsel-covered wires holding candles which are lighted as each of the Sundays in Advent pass. In other households Advent Calendars are bought or made, with small windows concealing scenes which are revealed, day by day, as the build-up to the exciting festival begins.

The actual date of Jesus's birthday was never established, although it was probably in April, and until nearly AD 400 different branches of the newly formed Christian Church celebrated this feast at different times of year. Because of all the traditional associations with the period after the winter solstice, especially as it was considered a time of hope and rebirth, the date of 25 December as Christ-mass was settled on by the church in Rome, in about AD 340. This happened to coincide with *Dies Natalis Invicti Solis*, the birth day of the Unconquered Sun, Mithras, who was originally a Persian God adopted by the Roman army, who constructed underground temples in his name wherever they went. Many of the ideas about the birth of Jesus, in a cave, surrounded by animals, actually hark back to the older secret tradition. The followers of Mithras, in the last 200 years or so BC, also had a communion meal of bread and wine, blessed as the body and blood of the sacrificed god.

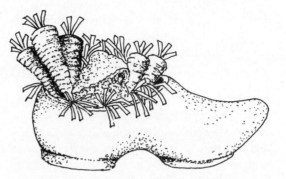

St Nicholas' Eve

In much of Europe, and particularly in Holland, the main fun takes place on St Nicholas' Eve, 5 December. According to the story, St Nicholas, who was a Bishop, comes each year in a ship from Spain, riding a white horse, to visit every child. To those who are good he will give a gift of sweets or biscuits, and those who have been bad get a light smack with a bunch of birch twigs. Children set out a clog or shoe beside the fireplace containing some hay, bread and a carrot to reward the saint's horse, in the hope that his assistant, Black Pete, will leave a present, rather than delivering a smack, or worse still, wrapping the really bad children up in the empty sack he carries and transporting them away to Spain as captives!

For this festival, presents are made rather than bought, and then disguised in well-wrapped parcels, each containing a poem or riddle about the person the present is for, but always signed 'St Nicholas' so that the recipient has to guess who sent what. These mysterious packages are piled in a special basket near the hearth. Late on the evening of 5 December there is a loud knocking or ringing at the door and when someone is sent to open it no visitor can be seen, only the basket of beautifully or ingeniously wrapped presents, which has been secretly placed there. Gifts may be small or large, but they have to be the kinds of things the recipient would really like; and the way they are disguised and the verse or riddle has to be aimed exactly at that person, reflecting his or her interests or hobbies. It is very much a matter of the thought that counts in this

tradition, and it really requires consideration and energy to make this festival a success. As the gifts are unwrapped, one at a time, to be admired, and the riddles are unravelled, it is a delight to see the faces both of the giver and the receiver.

Some gifts are taken to nearby friends' houses and delivered to the doorstep but the 'postman' has to ring the bell or knock and then run away so that it seems as though the present is given by a mysterious St Nicholas. There are lots of special songs, cakes and games at this time too, enjoyed by young and old alike. To really show how much you care about your family and friends in this way is a much more direct gift of love than some readymade, if expensive, present.

Mumming Plays

Another widespread custom which turns up throughout the Christmas period is the Mumming Play. These have many different local variations of character names, costumes and dialogue, but the traditional theme is one of a battle between the Goodies and Baddies, when even the Baddies who get slain in a fight are magically restored to life by a shamanic 'Doctor' figure. The play fulfils several important roles, not least of which is collecting some money for the Christmas Cheer of the players, or a local charity. In some places the actors are all men, often members of the local Morris Side, but in other places they may be a mixed group, or even school children, keeping up the old ways. It is meant to be funny, with slapstick humour and wild overacting by all concerned. The dialogue is usually in rhyming couplets or doggerel verse, and may be changed to accord with items or news, or to insult or make fun of individuals within the community.

The Yuletide version often begins with 'Father Christmas' opening the proceedings, which may be carried on out-of-doors, or in a pub or a house, or a public hall of some sort. He is not usually one of the combatants in the fight, but eggs on the Goodies and insults the Baddies and encourages the audience to join in, and finally part with as much money as possible. 'In comes I, Old Father Christmas, welcome or welcome not. I hope Old Father Christmas will never be forgot.' He gives way to the Hero of the story, Good George, King George or even St George who in turn has a mock sword fight with a variety of boastful challengers, like the Turkish, Moorish or plain Black Knight, whom he eventually 'kills' and knocks to the floor. There might be another fight from 'Bold Slasher' or in Sussex, the 'Turkey Snipe'! Sometimes even Beelzebub gets into the act with his words: 'In comes I, Beelzebub, in my hand I carries a club, in the other a frying pan, am I not a nasty old man?' He growls at the audience, scaring the children. There may be a Bessey, Betsy, Patsy or Beth, the disguised Man/Woman, often with a baby in tow, and a Fool with his traditional pig's bladder balloon on a stick, with which to harmlessly beat all participants or meaner members of the crowd.

The other central character to many versions of this old play is the Doctor, who like the rest of the cast has his moment of boasting, when the storytelling character calls 'Is there a Doctor to be found who can heal this dreadful wound?' and he bursts into the circle of players with his reply 'I can cure the itch, the stitch, the palsy and the gout, I can cure sickness from the inside out ...' and after much hamming produces from his bag or pocket a small medicine bottle from which he pours a life-restoring elixir down the throat of the dead victims, who in turn rise up and take their bow.

Around the main conflict dance the Hobby Horse and Fool, Father Christmas, the Betsy, and sometimes the musicians, who all attack the audience with their teeth, pig's bladder, ladle or club, according to character, and demand money from them! A 'Sweeper' or 'Whiffler' is sometimes present with a broom or whip to clear a space for the performance and to threaten anyone who looks like getting out of hand. In all, over nine hundred versions of this basic play have been recorded, some acted by characters with masks, some with blackened faces, some dressed in strips of rags or even paper, like the Marshfield Mummers from Gloucestershire who perform their play around a circuit of pubs on Boxing Day. Some groups have beautiful and elaborate outfits, others are in Morris dress, or ordinary clothes with signs painted on cardboard saying what they represent. In some versions of the story, the Betsy's child is a central figure, in others the Mumming play is part of Plough Monday celebrations, or the Easter 'Pace Egg' Play. In every version it is a celebration of the restoration of life that spring will bring in its wake. It is a rural celebration of joy, of the conquest of hard times and thanksgiving for benefits or blessings received.

Seasonal Greenery

Like many of the customs which have accreted around the Christmas season, most of those not directly derived from the New Testament story of the birth of Jesus have ancient or pagan roots. The gathering of greenery to deck houses is an extremely common part of seasonal festivals all over the world. In Britain, the most natural branches to use are those of the evergreens, the holly and the ivy, the fir and pine with their resinous and scented sap, and the mysterious mistletoe, sacred to the Druids, who sought it around the winter solstice, and carefully cut any such plants which they found on the oak tree. Most of the mistletoe we use to make Kissing Boughs and hang over the front door comes from apple, lime or poplar trees, although it will grow on many other species in the right conditions.

The Green Branch was always hung over the door indicating hospitality, and was one of the oldest signs of an inn, from which names like 'The Holly Bush' or 'The Greenwood Tree' have probably survived. A green branch was carried by heralds in battle, so it meant a ceasing of hostilities and a time for talk and reconciliation.

The holly with its sharp prickly leaves, pale flowers and blood-red berries, used for decoration long before the story of Jesus came to these islands, easily fitted into the folklore, and gave rise to the beautiful verses of the carol, 'The Holly and the Ivy'. The chorus, however, is certainly older in theme – 'The rising of the sun and the running of the deer,' seems to tie in with ancient hunting customs from the winter feast, whereas 'The playing of the merry organ and sweet singing in the choir' is obviously fairly modern. What the original line might have been has been speculated about by many pagan-hearted poets.

Another ancient custom linked to nature is the Yule Log. This again has its pagan connections, for wherever possible it was the root part of a large oak or possibly ash tree that was capable of being burned throughout the whole Twelve Days of Christmas and still having a bit over to kindle the next year's log. This harks back to the concept of the World Tree which supported the known universe in Saxon mythology, and from which Odin gained both power and knowledge. In some places from Kent to Somerset where a Yule Log cannot be found (for traditionally it shouldn't be bought) great bundles of ash branches or smaller logs are lashed together and burned as the 'Ashen Faggot'. The wood ash from the Yule Log was kept to be sprinkled over the fields as a kind of magical fertiliser.

The other tree which has become a standard part of the festival is the Christmas tree, made popular by Queen Victoria's husband, Albert, in whose native Germany it was customary to decorate trees at Yuletide. Introduced by the Royal Household, Christmas trees were fairly common all over the land by about 1840, including a huge outdoor one at Covent Garden, in London.

A decorated tree is a traditional part of winter celebrations in many other places, however. The idea of decorating a branch or a whole evergreen tree with lights, sweets, gifts and decorations is found all over the world, and has been reported as early as 2,000 BC in Mesopotamia, where beribboned branches were carried in procession in honour of the Gods and Goddesses of Fertility and Life. In the Roman Empire, green branches were hung with masks and artificial flowers in honour of Bacchus, the God of Wine.

Other decorative traditions include the Kissing Bough, made with mistletoe and greenery and

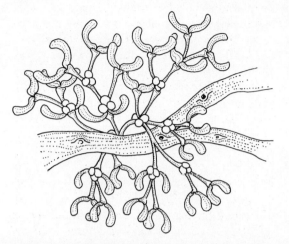

hung in the hallways of houses, under which guests could be greeted at the entrance. Like the Advent Crown this had candles upon it. There was also a Christingle made of interlocked hoops of cane or wire, mainly decorated with tinsel and coloured ribbons, and from it apples or red holly berries were usually hung. Candles upon branches, or on the table, even after the advent of gas and electric lighting in the home, would focus attention on the symbolism of the decorations. In Jewish households, the time around the winter solstice is celebrated as the Feast of Lights, and it is likely that some of the Christmas candles had this ancestry.

Saturnalia

The season of celebration around the winter solstice is very ancient, and in Roman times was dedicated to the Lord of Time, their God, Saturn, and known as Saturnalia. It was a time of reversal of roles; slaves were given a day off and served a meal by their masters, children could act like adults and give orders, and special foods were eaten. The ritual offering of burning candles, partly as magic to call back the sun, and partly to keep away any evil influences thought to be abroad at this dark time of year, was a common practice.

A small tradition has survived on this theme in the idea of the Boy Bishop, where these days a chosen chorister is allowed to take on the role of

Bishop, wear his cope and mitre, carry his crozier and participate in parts of the services where no ordained priest is necessary. Other children may assist during his brief 'reign'. This custom survives in Edwinstow in Nottinghamshire, Par in Cornwall, Bristol in Avon and near Bournemouth. In some places the Boy Bishop had to preach a sermon on Holy Innocents Day, at the end of his temporary office.

Seasonal Feasts

Special food has always been an important part of any celebration, and much of it becomes traditional because it is seasonal. There are lots of older versions of the things most people eat at Christmas. The pudding began as 'plum porridge', a more savoury dish, made with meat, breadcrumbs and dried fruit, and served as a sort of thick, cold soup at the start of the feast. Mincemeat, which we still have in mince pies, was also a savoury, with minced meat as well as the raisins, candied peel, suet and currants that are in modern mincemeat. This was cooked in a 'coffyn of paste', a pastry case, in the shape of a traditional crib. The puddings and pies and special dishes were cooked well before the event, often in late November on what was known as 'Stir up Sunday', when the reading in church on the last Sunday before Advent begins 'Stir up, we beseech thee, O Lord, the wills of thy faithful people ...' and this was taken as a hint to get on with the festive preparations. Many puddings used to contain small silver charms which were another form of luck-bringing or primitive prediction. The person who found the silver coin would gain money; the shoe or boot would mean travel; the tiny bell a wedding or other celebration like the birth of a child; and the horseshoe luck in general.

The main item of the old Christmas Feast was a whole roast sucking pig, or perhaps a decent-sized goose, stuffed with herbs, breadcrumbs and fruit, and carried into the packed dining room by sweating servants who didn't even get Christmas Day off. The turkey, which is so much a part of the christmas dinner now, is a latecomer to the feast, having been brought from America. It only found a place on the table in the last couple of decades. Before that, the smaller post-war households made their feast of chicken or pork in smaller quantities than the vast meals consumed by the extended families of Victorian times. Barons of beef, venison pasties, jugged hare, whole hams, game pies and vast cuts of every sort of edible animal, fish, bird or game creature found its way to the groaning boards of the wealthy at the end of the last century, and the kitchen staff would have been on their feet for days, preparing the pies, tarts, cakes and puddings, selecting fruits from the greenhouses and storerooms, and collecting every other vegetable or delicacy that could be provided. The poor in the streets and workhouses, on the other hand, would be lucky to get hot gruel and a loaf of stale bread.

Cards and Crib Scenes

Christmas cards, which now seem to appear in shops as soon as the July Sales have finished, were again a Victorian idea, developed from about 1845, but becoming more widespread by 1870. Early designs show the robin redbreast, a bird familiar in our gardens in the winter, and already associated with Jesus's death at Easter, having acquired his red breast feathers by trying to pull out the thorns from the Messiah's head. Printing methods allowed colours to be added, and nowadays there are sparkles, three dimensional effects, and anti-Christmas cards for those fed up with the hype and vulgarity. The Green Movement is producing recycled cards, preferably to be delivered by hand, on foot, or by bicycle, to the recipient, in which case the old tradition of actually meeting and greeting your loved ones at this holy time would be restored.

In many churches, and at charity collecting points, there is often a crib scene among the greenery. This too is an ancient tradition going back to the worship of the Mother Goddess Isis who was depicted seated nursing her son, Horus, in both public and private shrines. Making models of holy scenes with natural materials such as wood, straw, clay or flowers turn up all over the world. The making or setting up of the traditional nativity of Jesus, with the Virgin Mary and Joseph, the shepherds, and the various animals in their primitive shelter, stable or cave can be a moving time for all concerned. It brings the scene so much more closely to heart than any amount of pious words or television documentaries. Mithras, the dying and reviving God whose birthday also falls on 25 December, was born in a cave, surrounded by a bull and a dog, a lion and often a snake, in representation of the four elements of life.

Symbols of Rebirth

The whole tradition of a God born in the middle of winter is a widespread and ancient theme, based on the return of the power of the Sun, which in many lands is seen as a symbol of the Male God, although there is a deep-seated principle that as the sun is the giver of life, she could be a Goddess. In many ceremonies within the church and among modern pagans there is a moment of pitch darkness when a new spark is kindled in the old way of striking iron on flint. From this, one candle is lit, and from that a ripple of light goes through the whole place, each person receiving the reborn light. It is a time of hope and of promise, and the Child of the Year is known as the Star Child, which is still echoed in the Epiphany theme of the Magi following the star to Bethlehem.

It has been said that many people have died because of their belief in Jesus and the Christian faith but no one has died for believing in Father Christmas. Santa Claus or Father Christmas is another figure brought into the midwinter celebrations from an older and more Northern Tradition. His reindeer might give us a clue that, again, this white bearded, red-coated figure is another Sun God in the guise of a gift bringer and life restorer, coming south on his sleigh loaded with presents from the far north. The Fairy at the top of the Christmas Tree, just like the statue of Mary in the Crib Scene, is a Holy Mother, recognised in all customs which also honour the Son. She offers the greatest gift of all, Life Everlasting in the sacrificial offering of her sacred Son, whether his name is Jesus, or Attis, or Mithras.

The glittering tinsel, the coloured lights or flickering candles illuminating the Christmas

table, the mysterious, gaily wrapped presents under the tree, the lumpy stocking at the end of the bed on Christmas morning, the piles of cards falling on to the doormat for weeks, the food and good cheer, the green branches, trailing ivy, strange mistletoe – all these have ancient roots. This was perhaps the most sacred of all the seasons for this festival, celebrated a few days after the longest night, or the shortest day of the winter solstice, proved that the light of the sun would return. The Sun/Son was reborn in the cave of winter and even if the weather grew colder and more bleak, spring would follow. When you hold this feast, in whatever way you go about it, in church, in your home, or in some other-than-Christian temple, remember all those who have lost the light of hope, and in the candle glow send out good wishes for a brighter future for all upon this Earth we share.

Boxing Day

The sacrifice theme is not entirely absent from the Yuletide days, for on St Stephen's Day, or

Boxing Day, there is an old, and fortunately now quite rare, tradition of 'Hunting the Cutty Wren'. From Wales to the Isle of Mann and in Ireland Wren Boys would seek out this tiny brown victim, pin its small corpse to a bier and carry it through the streets. Sometimes the wren was caught, and either caged for the rest of the Twelve Days of Christmas, or decked out in tiny ribbons and then set free. There are several songs or chants attached to this seemingly pointless hunt, one goes:

> The wren, the wren, the King of all birds,
> On St Stephen's day was caught in the furze,
> Though he be little his honour is great,
> Therefore Good People, give us a treat.

and in exchange for a glance at the small victim, sweets, cakes or any other gifts were offered to the Wren Boys. There is another song which tells of the capture of the Cutty Wren, which has to be cooked in '... a ruddy great brass cauldron'. Each verse of the song indicated that the dish of the day was a huge and important thing, not the tiny, innocent bird.

Boxing Day has other, nicer connotations, for

it was then that the Servants, Apprentices and, to this day, people who bring a service to our doors, like Paper Boys or Girls, Milkmen, Refuse Removal Officers and Postal Delivery Operatives, get a tip, usually money. In earlier times the Box after which the day is named had two forms. One was a money box, often made of clay, into which alms were sought by apprentices from the customers they served. Only at the appropriate moment could this hard receptacle be broken open. The other was a box of clothing, material or food given to servants attached to a large house who had been working their fingers to the bone over the holiday. Sometimes the staff were given the day off to visit their families and take them presents of useful things, such as cast-off clothing from the 'Big House', or food from the Christmas Feast.

Hogmanay

As if the feasting and activities of Christmas were not enough at this chilly and dark time of year, there is also the festival, at the end of the month, of New Year's Eve, or 'Hogmanay'. Because it is only the civil calendar which begins on 1 January

Hogmanay has not been such an important celebration in Christmas-conscious England, although parties are held here where everyone stays up to hear the New Year rung in with bells, and in many places fireworks are let off, and other noisy ways of welcoming the New Year take place.

Scotland has always made more of the New Year feast than England does, and has a variety of customs associated with it. Some of the customs continue the theme of divination at those turning points in a year when it is thought that information might be available. One tradition is that of Bibliomancy, wherein the Family Bible is prayed over and then the person seeking his fortune opens it at random, marking a verse with his finger. Whatever that verse discusses will be his fortune for the year. Others seek out predictions from weather lore at this hinge moment of the calendar year, looking out of doors at midnight, to see which way the wind is blowing:

> If New Year's Eve night-wind blows south,
> That betokens warmth and growth.
> If west, much milk and fish in the sea,
> If north much cold and storms will be.
> If east, the trees will bear much fruit,
> If north-east, flee it, man and brute.

SAGITTARIUS, THE ARCHER

Those who have birthdays in early December may suffer as children the sadness of seldom having both birthday presents and Christmas presents or parties. They are ruled by the fiery sign, Sagittarius, the strange half horse, half archer, or centaur with a bow and arrow, and by the generous planet Jupiter, and are kindly and outgoing people on the whole. They are humane, friendly, strong-willed and independent, and make excellent, if often put-upon, companions. They are honest, hard working and responsible, but have a volatile sense of the absurd and can seem to change direction in their life style unexpectedly. They are often deeply religious, but not necessarily in a conventional form, seeing the value of a moral standpoint, or a spiritual aspect to life which may be ignored by other people. They are sincere, frank and sometimes painfully outspoken in company, but can also be philosophical and thoughtful. The writers Jonathan Swift and Thomas Carlyle, and the poet John Milton were Sagittarians, as was the mysterious prophet 'Nostradamus', the philosopher Spinoza, and the composers Ludwig van Beethoven, and Weber.

Sagittarians are very sporting types, on the whole, enjoying outdoor pursuits in keeping with the Horse/Hunter which is part of the Archer's make up. They like animals, preferring the larger ones to small pets, and in earlier times, perhaps enjoying the hunting of big game. They are gamblers too, watching horse racing for their joy in the horses, but also because of their gaming instincts and shrewd desire to place lucky bets. They are adventurous, leading parties up the Orinoco or into deepest Wiltshire, questing for new knowledge or a valuable prize, but they do expect their friends to play by the rules and not cheat.

Romantically they can be difficult, for they tend to be idealistic, changeable and sometimes impractical, wishing their partners to fulfil some dream-like activity which just doesn't work out in real life. They do have many excellent features though, mainly to do with the old fashioned ideas of charm, gentlemanly behaviour, (and this applies equally to the Ladies of the Sign), and good humour. They make enchanting friends, being garulous, generous and imaginative, although this may be trying to quieter people. They have a strange, almost mystical religious outlook, or follow some humanist philosophy to great lengths.

The colours which suit this winter sign include muted ambers, burnt orange, and many forms of deep blue, purple, paler mauves and greys. They are active people, loving the countryside and animals, especially horses because of their 'centaur' connection, and dogs, as adjuncts to their hunting and archery skills. They like to dress in variations on country clothes or those really designed for riding or other sporting occasions, so may choose natural browns, greens and wild flower colours rather than bright ones. The jewels which they like best include sapphires and amethysts, but many of the other stones with blue or purple forms, such as aquamarines, deep rose quartz or lapis lazuli and turquoise, please them.

DECEMBER RECIPES

Jugged Hare

1 hare
4 carrots
3 small onions
2 oz/60g/¼ cup butter
2 tbsp flour
6 rashers streaky bacon
2 small glasses red wine
drop of port
1 bayleaf, salt and pepper
approximately 1 pint/ 60cl/2½ cups good
   brown stock or marinade liquid
2 oz/60g/½ cup arrowroot (optional)
2 tbsp redcurrant jelly
Marinade
1 large glass sweet cider
1 large glass white vinegar
1 onion, sliced, salt and pepper

Hang the hare for three to four days, then skin and joint it. The day before you cook the jugged hare, mix the marinade ingredients in a large bowl and steep the hare joints in the mixture.

Peel and chop the vegetables. Melt the butter in a frying pan, brown the vegetables and transfer to a large casserole. Coat the hare joints in the flour and fry until slightly browned. Lay the hare pieces on top of the vegetables, and the rashers of bacon on top of these. Pour over the wine and stock and add the bayleaf and salt and pepper. Cook, covered, in a 350°F/180°C/Mark 4 oven for about three hours. If the sauce is too thin, thicken it with the arrowroot. Just before serving, add the redcurrant jelly.

Red Cabbage Dish

This is the traditional red cabbage accompaniment for the festive bird (or nut loaf!).

½ small red cabbage
1 large bramley apple
1 onion
1 tbsp vinegar
1 tbsp red wine or water

Slice the cabbage, apple and onion into similar-sized pieces, and place in a saucepan with a tightly fitting lid, or a lidded casserole dish if you want to bake it in the oven. Add the vinegar and wine or water. Simmer the cabbage on top of the stove for about an hour or place in a preheated 300°F/150°C/Mark 2 oven for roughly two hours. The cabbage mixture should be a delicate shade of purple, and not too soft in texture.

Gluhwein Recipe

Gluhwein is a German drink that is served hot and is therefore ideal for winter parties.

3 bottles dry red wine
½ bottle brandy
½ pint/30cl/1⅓ cups orange juice
rind and juice of 2 lemons
½ pint/30cl/1⅓ cups water
1 orange stuck with 12 cloves
6 cinnamon sticks

Place all the ingredients in a large cooking pot and simmer for about 20 minutes.

Brandysnaps

Brandysnaps are an excellent Yuletide treat, and make a highly acceptable gift.

2 oz/60g/¼ cup butter
2 oz/60g/⅓ cup brown sugar
2 tbsp golden syrup
2 oz/60g/½ cup flour
2 tsp ground ginger
pinch of salt
2 tbsp brandy or lemon juice

Melt the butter in a saucepan with the sugar and syrup. Sift in the flour and add the ginger, salt and brandy or lemon juice, if using. Drop tablespoons of the mixture well apart on thoroughly greased baking trays. Place in a preheated 350°F/180°C/Mark 4 oven for about seven minutes, until golden brown. Cool them just enough to handle, then shape them round a spoon handle.

A WILDLIFE CHRISTMAS TREE

In the autumn, start to collect seeds, berries, nuts, hips and haws, in preparation for this midwinter feast for the birds and other wildlife. 'Bird Cake' can be made from seeds, nuts, bread and dried fruits, set in fat in used yogurt pots: knot one end of a piece of string and thread the other end through the base of the yogurt pot, to form a hanging 'bell'. Mix the dry ingredients with melted fat and spoon into the pot; leave to set. Another treat for the birds is peanuts in their shells, threaded on to lengths of twine with a large, blunt needle.

Having collected the foodstuffs, you need somewhere to hang them. Find a large branch from a tree and choose a place in your garden, or outside a window, where it can be firmly anchored in the ground or fixed to a support. When the really cold weather comes, attach the bells of bird cake and the peanut strings to the branch. Also tie on the stems of berries, wild fruits, hips and haws still attached to their twigs.

During the coldest part of winter, when need for food will overcome some of the wilder birds' fears, you will find all kinds feeding at this special branch. The seeds that fall to the ground will nourish other creatures. Please also find a way to put out shallow bowls of fresh, clean water where birds can not only drink but, even in very cold weather, can paddle and bathe. An old frying pan is good, and any ice can be easily turned out to be replaced with fresh water. You may be amazed at what kinds of wildlife there are in the most suburban setting.

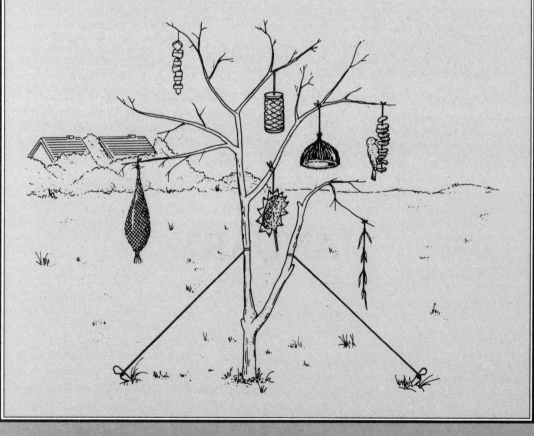

JANUARY

A Kindly good Janiveer freezeth the pot by the fire
Country saying

Welcoming in the New Year

The New Year is rung in with the sweet bells chiming at midnight after the muffles from their clappers that rang out the Old Year have been removed. Many things are welcomed with rituals to bring luck, to ward off harm in the coming season and to celebrate the moment of change. Traditionally luck was brought into the house in a variety of ways. In Scotland an old custom involves the first bucket of water drawn from a well on New Year's Day. As there could only be one 'first' bucket it was called the 'Cream' or 'Flower' of the well, which might have been shared by several families, so there was a minor contest by all concerned to bring in this beneficial water. Sometimes water was brought from a ford between the village and burial ground, both on New Year's Eve, as water of the dead, and then New Year's Morning as the water of life.

This was sprinkled around the house and sipped by all present to ensure health. In some communities the whole house was sealed up, and then scented and aromatic branches such as Juniper were burned, making much smoke, to fumigate the home and drive out any lurking nasties. Byres and stables were similarly treated. Here both water and fire are used to cleanse and bless the home for the people and livestock, in exactly the same way that these symbols are used in many beneficial religious rites. In Wales the special water was contested for but it was used to wash the dairy utensils and given to cows and calves to drink, in order to increase the milk yield.

There are also welcoming ceremonies, whereby one door is opened and all bad luck swept out, although it is normally not done to sweep straight out of the door; and then the opposite door to the house is opened and good luck and blessings called in. There is a Welsh poem which invites the 'Fair maid, with gold upon her toe who drives out the old', and 'Fair maid with gold upon her chin, Open up the East door and let the new year in'.

The custom which many people in Scotland and much of England are familiar with is that of 'First Footing' when a dark-haired man (women entering at this critical moment are seen, in some

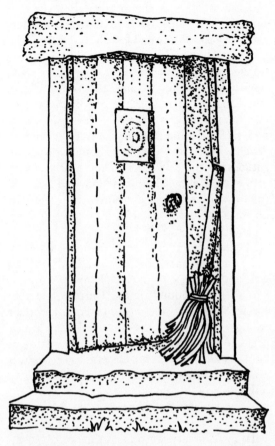

communities, as harbingers of doom) comes to the door immediately after midnight. This gentleman should be handsome, with especially high-arched feet, and in most places definitely dark haired, although, like all taboos which are broken on one special date, in Bradford in Yorkshire redhaired men, usually scorned as unchancy, are the preferred form of 'First Footers'. Anyone who had a squint, was lame or otherwise disfigured was definitely not acceptable and anyone known to be mean or tight fisted wouldn't have been welcome either. The First Footer should not be wearing black or be in mourning, nor carry anything sharp pointed nor bring any kind of unkind thoughts, which one way or another seemed to have ruled out most of the population!

Not only did each region specify what the First Footer was to look like and wear, but it also determined what his gifts to the house should consist of. Nearly everywhere he was expected to bring a lump of coal, (or peat, firewood, or kindling) a loaf of bread (or special cake or bicuits) and a bottle of whiskey (or beer, mead or wine). He might also carry a branch of green leaves, the traditional sign of a messenger. He would enter in silence and then individually wish everyone in the house 'A Happy New Year'. He might, if he were tuneful, sing a carol like:

I wish you a merry Christmas, a Happy New Year,
A pocketful of money and a cellar full of beer,
A good fat pig to last you all the year,
So please give me a gift for the New Year.

In Scotland one of the presents might be a red herring, and in Wales there is a custom of dressing an apple by sticking into it ears of corn, cloves, rosemary (the traditional herb of remembrance), and nuts and evergreen leaves. This 'Calennig' apple was brought into the house and set up on a stand of holly or rowan twigs. Sometimes the offering was gilded or decked with gay ribbons. In Scotland, one possible origin of the word 'Hogmanay', literally 'gift cake', from the Norman French, is the name of a triangular oat cake or shortbread made for the occasion, to be eaten with Christmas cheese. Every one of these symbolic acts or gifts has ancient roots which show that no matter what the season, there are customs to ensure luck, health, food and drink, and the cheer of good company. On each occasion these blessings have to be worked for and invited in; and the taboos of the time must be carefully observed. The rituals show the renewal and continuance of a pact with Nature to work hand in hand for the benefits of the house, its people, the farmyard and the livestock, the fields, meadows and orchards, and all that worked in or on them.

The first week of January is still part of the Twelve Days of Christmas, and in earlier times the feasting and merry making would be continuing, all in celebration of the lengthening days and growing light. Prognostications about the weather were made, depending on the temperature, direction of the wind and any rain or snow, for it was felt that the Twelve Days might represent the twelve months of the year, so if it was dry it would suggest a dry spring or summer, if wet, then not such helpful weather might befall.

the star, which was almost certainly a conjunction of bright planets, were led to the place where the baby Jesus, Mary and Joseph were camping in a stable. They brought gifts of Gold for Earthly sovereignty, Frankincense for holiness, and Myrrh for sacrifice to offer the young Christ. The Kings, Caspar, Melchior and Balthazar, one of whom is usually depicted as being dark-skinned, have gained a place in the tradition and on Twelfth Night they are placed in the Crib as substitutes for the shepherds. They nearly always gain a place in the Children's Nativity Plays, and the way in which their horses or camels or donkeys are shown is a trial of mothers' ingenuity.

Epiphany is a time of revelation, for it was by this visit from the Kings that the Birth of Jesus was voiced abroad to the people of the world. It was their honouring of the Christ Child that accepted him into the world of flesh, and their telling of the story as they returned home which began to spread knowledge of this incarnation of God. In the Greek and Eastern Churches this time is known as 'Hemera ton Photon', the Day of Light, and St Augustine declared it was 'God manifesting himself by the miracle of human nature'.

To the ordinary person it is time to put away the Christmas tinsel, pack up the tangle of tree lights, the crumpled sheets of wrapping paper saved for next year, take down the cards, the greenery and decorations and try to scrape the children's snowy stencils from the windows. In earlier times there was a verse to mark this time:

Down with the Rosemary and Bayes, Down with
    the Mistletoe
Instead of Holly now up-raise the greener Box
    for show.

In substitute for the lack of brightness many people tried to find a few flowers, even weeds like shepherd's purse or groundsel, which might be flowering early in sheltered spots, if the snow was not covering the land, and the green box leaves, not normally a part of the Yuletide decorations, were substituted for the more traditional evergreens. It was also the end of the Yule Log, now frequently only seen as a small chocolate cake substitute in homes with central heating. The last

Any signs of flowers, greenery or other growth were observed with interest, and preparations were made for the first of the early lambs. One of the flowers looked for at this time of year is the blossoming of the Holy Thorn of Glastonbury, and the Christmas Rose or Black Hellebore, which is poisonous.

Because of the changes made to the calendar in 1752 to bring England into line with Europe, some festivals have two dates, one being about eleven days later than its modern counterpart. It often seems that the activities of Nature are out of step with the day attributed to them by the modern calendar. For example, May Day, the day on which hawthorn is usually seen in bloom, seems to fall about 12 May, although in recent warm, dry springs, it has actually been blossoming earlier. It also means that some feasts or activities traditionally linked with the Christmas season have moved back into mid-January. This period of dark and dull days was sometimes known as the 'Dismal' although this term originally referred to the times of plague or the Ides in each month of the Roman calendar, about which the augurs or oracles would warn their clients to beware.

Epiphany

The last feast of the Christmas Twelve Days is Epiphany, when, according to folk tradition rather than the Gospels, the Three Kings, led by

chunk of a big tree root would be hidden away in a dry place until next Christmas, but the ashes which had been raked out of the hearth would have to be saved, for soon it would be Plough Monday, when the first furrow would be cut and the healing and fertility-promoting ash would be sprinkled on the land.

King Boggan

In some places, a Twelfth Night Cake is baked before the end of the feast and it is usual to include a dried pea and a dried bean so that the man and woman who each receive one of these tokens become King Bean and Queen Pea for the last day of revels, which were often as important as Christmas Day itself. It is another day on which the Medieval Mummers took their tales of combat, death and revival to the houses and village greens, often dressed with animal heads, according to old manuscript pictures. In Lincoln-shire the King Bean has become King Boggan, who is the Master of Revels at some ancient and possibly sacrificial rites in the village of Haxey. He is dressed in a tall hat, decorated with blood red flowers and carries thirteen willow wands, bound with thirteen bands, perhaps as a symbol of the thirteen Lunar months in the year. A Fool is the victim of the start of the rite, when he stands on the remains of the village cross and tells a story of Lady de Mowbray who left land the

rent from which should be used in perpetuity to reward some game men who went to the rescue of her scarlet hood, blown off by a fierce wind. That is the modern version, but as he tells this tale, the paper streamers on the back of the black-faced Fool's costume are set alight, and damp straw and rags about his feet set to smoulder, so 'Smoking the Fool'. The King Boggan throws one of a set of 'hoods' made of canvas to the crowd and the catcher has to run to the nearest pub without being caught by the King Boggan or one of his assistants. Eleven more hoods are thrown and those which reach an inn in safety earn the catcher a small money prize. Finally a red leather hood is brought into play, and a huge scrum of people descends on it, each trying to grab the hood and carry it to safety in one of the three pubs, where all gain free drinks then, and the hood is kept for another year. Though there is lots of pushing and shoving most of these winter games result in few serious injuries, and it is honour rather than any kind of valuable prize which is at stake.

Plough Monday

Work starts again and Plough Monday is a signal to all the agricultural labourers to get over the holiday and set to work to till the land, if conditions are favourable. The old fashioned horse plough would be decorated with ribbons and artificial flowers and those attending it wore bright costumes with paper streamers and anything else colourful. The plough was dragged by the ploughmen into the church for the priest to bless with holy water and incense. It might be pulled through the streets as those accompanying it begged for alms, to keep candles burning in front of farming saints, or local ones. Those who were mean on this occasion might find their path ploughed up, their dung heap scattered or front garden furrowed by the displeased ploughboys.

The oxen or 'stots' were sometimes garlanded and led through the streets, accompanied by Morris or Sword Dances. In East Anglia there was a Straw Bear figure led through the streets at this time too. Mumming Plays were put on and similar final opportunities for dressing up and playing the Fool were taken, before the really hard work of the year began.

Mari Lwyd

In Wales they have a particular and singular tradition between Yule and about the middle of January, which is the custom involving the 'Mari Lwyd', the white mare. Once again the ghost horse makes its appearance at an ancient festival, in this case the skull of a real horse is fixed on to a pole and decked out with bells, ribbons and a kind of canvas hood which covers the head of the man underneath. This mysterious beast is accompanied by Punch and Judy, a Sergeant and a musician called the Merryman. They call at houses and a kind of verbal dual in Welsh ensues, wherein the 'Mari Lwyd' party ask permission to sing their song within the house, but those within answer, in verse, with questions about who is outside and their names. It is a challenge of insults shouted through the door, and as 'Judy' is often the largest man in the parish, and the Mari Lwyd has snapping jaws and glittering eyes, they are a fearful party to turn away. Eventually they are allowed into the house where they attack and jostle the folk within, Punch chasing and kissing the women present and Judy beating the rest with a hearth broom she carries. After this minor battle, food and drink are offered to the party and the singing of traditional songs, carols and even

dancing, space permitting, continues for some time. In the end the Mari Lwyd party offer a final verse of benediction to the house, and set off to harass some other household. The riddle song or insults and the horse are echoes of the same idea carried out in Padstow, when the black 'Obby 'Oss first comes out, singing the Night Song under the windows of the townsfolk.

January sees the stirrings of life on the land, and the horse may be garlanded with the first yellow blooms of forsythia and dark green box leaves, sometimes substituted in churches for Druidic mistletoe. In really sheltered areas where the snow has stayed away there may well be the first white faces of daisies dotting the winter lawns and in wilder spots the spikey teasel heads, no longer gathered to tease wool strands in the carding process, linger unwanted. Ivy has its black berries and fragrant pine cones may be gathered to light the New Year fires.

Wassailing the Trees

The apple, its tree and blossom all have important symbolic connections in Celtic folklore; for example, the place to which heroes go after death, to await restoration and return, is the Isle of Avalon, the Apple Isle. Many customs concerning apples are still practised today. In those parts of the country – Somerset, Kent and Herefordshire – where cider orchards still stand, there is an old custom of Wassailing the trees, on about 17 January (Old Twelfth Night). This ritual, now usually done by the local Morris side, is intended to bless the trees to make them fruitful and to drive away harm from them in the coming year. After dark, men with shotguns, others with slices of toast, jugs of cider and things to make a noise with, gather in the orchards. In some cases a child was lifted up into the chosen tree, usually the largest in the orchard, and given something to eat and drink. In other places the guns were discharged through the branches and tin cans and trays were beaten to ward off harm. Libations of cider were poured over the tree roots and pieces of bread or toast, soaked in cider, were placed in the branches. Each region has its own wassailing song; in Sussex they have the following version:

Stand fast root, bear well top,
Pray God send us a howling good crop,
On every twig, apples big, on every bough,
apples enow.
Hats full, caps full, great quarter-sacks full,
Holla boys, holla! Hazza!

Other fruiting trees were also wassailed in a similar manner, and the custom is maintained as far away as Normandy, famous for its cider brandy, Calvados. Here, sometimes, small fires of straw are lit below the trees and lighted torches are thrown through their branches. Singing songs to trees or exhorting them to fruition was carried out under pear, fig, cherry, hazel and walnuts, as well as many of the fruiting bushes, such as currants and gooseberries, and offerings of watered cider or ale were poured on them too.

Fire Festivals

Noise and fire are common parts of many winter customs, and in Scotland there are several daring and exciting events in January, to welcome the New Year and make offerings for continued prosperity and luck. One, in Burghead, Morayshire, a fishing seaport, involves burning the 'Clavie' – a barrel, cut in parts and full of broken staves and tar, which has been ignited with hot peat. Custom says that none of the tools used, either in the cutting of the barrel or the nailing it to a pole for carrying, may be bought; so a stone is used instead of a hammer and the nails are made by a smith. The ignited Clavie is carried through the town and round the harbour by the Clavie King. Pieces of the burning wood are thrown into houses to bring good fishing or fortune to those chosen for this dubious gift. The Clavie is used to light a great bonfire made up of broken barrels on the headland overlooking the sea and eventually it is rolled down a hill. Fragments of the burned Clavie are sought to light house fires, again to ward off the attentions of evil spirits and ensure a year of luck. No one knows the origins of this firesome rite, whether it be from the Norse invaders, the Celtic Druids or simply ancient superstition; however, like other blazes, it is thought to continue to bring success and health to the community.

In Shetland, in Lerwick, again around this time of year, is an even more dramatic Fire Festival, the 'Up-Helly-Aah!' Here it is a replica Viking Ship which is the sacrificial victim of the New Year custom. It might be a memorial to some long-forgotten Viking King who was sent forth to his resting place in Valhalla in a blazing ship, or it may just be an offering to the Sea Gods to be kind and generous to the fisherfolk. For over a month, led by the Chief Guiser (or in Norse, the Guiser Jarl), the three hundred or so participants in this northern isle construct the thirty-foot model of the Norse Longship, with its banners, heraldic shields and oars. Many are dressed as Vikings, in mail and with horned or winged helmets. Other Guisers dress in different kinds of costumes, nightshirts, historial costumes and all manner of odd get-ups. There are bands to accompany the great ship as it is pulled through the streets towards the sea.

Many of the participants have been extremely secretive about their costumes and the acts which they intend to play out in the various halls around the town, before dawn. With the Jarl at the helm and his body guard of Vikings the whole procession goes through the town to the place of immolation, followed by all the guisers carrying tall, flaming torches. At the end, the Vikings leave the ship and a circle of torches rings it, before they are cast into it at a bugle call. As it blazes away the crowd sings 'The Norseman's Home'. As it flames to a redhot end about fifty gangs of guisers visit as many of the halls as possible, performing their acts, eating and drinking until well after dawn the next day.

Burns' Night

It would seem that in the North there are more early January customs and old traditions because in the south of England people are still recovering from the over-indulgences of Christmas, and preparing themselves for the January Sales, which now seem to celebrate commercial values earlier and earlier each year. Some now start at the end of December. Scotland celebrates not only life and fire, but the works and life of its foremost poet, Robbie Burns. Robert Burns was born in

1759 and his many lowlands, or in the dialect in which much of it tends to be delivered, 'Lallans' verses have become popular with the common folk in Scotland and all over the world. His poem about a mouse, 'Wee, sleekit, cowrin' tim'rous beastie,' and his famous words, '... would God the giftie gie us, to see ourselves as others see us!' are often quoted.

On 25 January there is an especially Scottish feast, even if it is eaten in Robbie Burns' honour the world over, with a sheep's head soup, called 'Powsowdie', wind-dried cod with horseradish sauce, called 'Cabbie-claw' and of course, the centrepiece of many a Scots dinner, the Haggis. Burns even wrote about that traditional dish: 'Fair fa' your honest, sonsie face, Great chieftain o' the puddin race!' This filling speciality is made by stuffing a sheep's stomach with minced offal, mutton, oatmeal and spices, and boiling the pudding. It is served, usually having been 'piped' in by a bagpiper, by being cut open with a Saint Andrew's cross, and the savoury filling dished out. It is often eaten with 'mashed neeps',

actually swede, and potatoes. Robbie Burns provided a Grace to say at the start of the meal 'Some hae meat that canna eat, And some wad eat that want it, But we hae meat and we can eat, Sae let the Lord be thankit!' To herald the various toasts that follow the meal there is another verse ending '... Let Meg noo tak' awa the flesh and Jock bring in the spirit!'

Those who are steeped in Burns' famous lines will do their best to quote them, and some stalwart souls have managed to commit the whole of 'Tam o'Shanter' to mind. Others, of more southerly aspect, content themselves with drinking the interminable toasts, enduring the patriotic and sentimental speeches, often from exiles from Scotland, and awaiting that most familiar of Burns' songs, 'Auld Lang Syne'. 'Should Auld Acquaintance be forgot and never brought to mind, we'll take a cup and drink it up, for the sake of Auld Land Syne!' Part of many people's New Year Celebrations, yet particularly special on Burns' own Night.

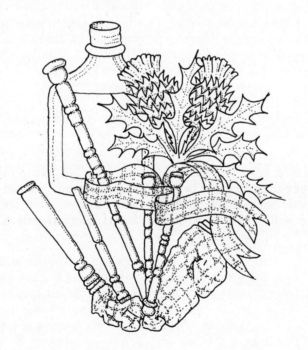

CAPRICORN, THE SEAGOAT

For those with birthdays over Christmas and into the New Year, the sign of the zodiac is Capricorn, the Seagoat, ruled by the dark but enduring planet, Saturn, between the winter solstice on 21 December and 21 January. Capricorns strive to reach the highest peaks of achievement, like their animal counterparts, who dwell in high places. They are idealists, lovers of freedom, both of body and spirit, and often tread a path which sets them apart from their contemporaries. Sir Isaac Newton and Johann Kepler, the astronomer, and Joan of Arc were born under this sign and show extremes of various sorts which is typical of the Capricorn character. Although they tend to have their feet on the ground and are practical people, they do like to look back at the past, or follow studies or occupations with a historical, archaeological or folkloric aspect. They are patient, reserved, quiet and even secretive, hating display or over-effusiveness, but they are loyal and determined, long-suffering and shrewd, and can seem shy for they are slow to trust. They do not suffer fools gladly and though slow to anger, can smoulder with resentment and plot extremely nasty revenge, although they are far too gentle to actually carry out these acts of vengeance.

As those ruled by Saturn they may be slow to develop, being pale and miserable children. They may develop well in later life when all the advantages of having this Lord of Time (Saturn's other name is Chronos) as an overseer of life reveal themselves. Their friendship can be extremely valuable, even if it takes a long time to develop, and for people who keep their word, they are extremely reliable. They can be prone to leg troubles, or joint pain, or have sensitive skin, which is often pale, especially if they have characteristically dark hair and eyebrows.

Like the other Signs ruled by Saturn, they are people who like their own company, and are content being left to enjoy their own kind of music on a personal stereo, or having their nose buried in a book. They don't often seek approval of others but can be tenacious in pursuit of a prize or job which they consider worth the effort of winning. Because of their ambitions they can become anxious as they are not folk who easily share any burdens, either physical or mental. They can be patient, hoping to out-wait others seeking the same end, but by the same token, can seem selfish or self-centred. They are often lonely people, suffering from natural reserve and shyness, coupled with suspicion of the motives of others or of any outward display of emotion. Their self-discipline and restraint can be legendary, but if they have set personal sights on a peak of achievement heaven help those who might stand in their path. They have the goat's headstrong way of butting others out of their chosen way.

The colours which suit these sombre folk may include black, dark purple, violet and many of the darker shades of blue, green and red. They look well in rich textures and deep, intense colours, and can appear stunning in plain black and white outfits suiting the quite formal occasions which they will favour. Greys, from a pale shimmering silver to deep charcoal, will be effective, highlighted with touches of colour, or simply a flower buttonhole or corsage. The jewels which may appeal to them are all dark – obsidian, onyx and jet – but large, dark stones of many of the gems and extravagant diamond pieces might suit them on occasion, for they do like the good things in life.

Venison Stew

Mutton from a shoulder or leg can be used as an alternative to venison in this recipe.

2 lb/1kg/5 cups trimmed, cubed venison
1 oz/30g/½ cup plain flour
2 tbsp vegetable oil
2 onions, coarscly chopped
squeeze lemon juice
1 glass port
½ pint/30cl/1⅓ cups beef stock
4 juniper berries
salt and black pepper

Season the flour with salt and pepper. Roll the cubes of venison in the flour. Put the oil in a heavy casserole and fry the onion until it starts to brown. Then add the meat, turning the pieces over as they brown. Add the lemon juice, port, stock and juniper berries and any remaining flour. Season, cover and simmer for 1½ hours or until tender. Serve with baked potatoes and redcurrant or rowanberry jelly.

Philip's Festive Fruit Cake

This is a wonderful cake which can be served at any festive occasion, including Epiphany.

8 oz/250g/2 cups plain flour
½ tsp baking powder
1 tsp mixed spice
6 oz/175g/1 (firmly packed) cup soft brown
   sugar
6 oz/175g/¾ cup hard margarine, softened
3 large eggs, beaten
1 lb/500g/3 cups mixed dried fruit, soaked
   overnight in tea, wine or apple juice
2 oz/60g/¼ cup glacé or candied cherries
Optional additions: chopped or whole nuts,
   raisins, crystallised ginger, or soaked dried
   apple rings or apricots

Mix, in a blender if you have one, the flour, baking powder, spice and sugar. Add the margarine and blend it in, then add the eggs and blend again. Put the soaked dried fruit, cherries and any 'extras' you fancy into a large bowl. Gradually add the flour and egg mixture to the bowl, mixing everything together thoroughly.

Grease and line with paper a 7 inch/18 centimetre cake tin. If you like, line the bottom of the tin with soaked apple rings. Pour the cake mixture into the tin and top, if desired, with an arrangement of almonds and Brazil nuts. Place the cake in a preheated 325°F/170°C/Mark 3 oven for 2 to 2½ hours, testing to see that it is cooked by inserting a skewer into it (the skewer should emerge clean).

Allow the cake to cool on a rack. There is so much fruit in this cake that it can't all sink to the bottom!

As part of the Twelfth Night Celebrations it was traditional to bake a rich fruit cake containing one bean and one pea. The man who received the slice containing the bean was chosen as King Bean for the evening revels, and the lady who found the pea was chosen as Queen.

Lamb's Wool

Lamb's Wool is a seasonal drink and the perfect accompaniment for fruit cake.

3 pints/1.75 litres/7 cups brown ale
1 bottle sweet white wine
1 tsp each grated nutmeg, ground ginger and
   cinnamon
2 baked apples
brown sugar to taste

Pour the ale and wine into a large pan, add the spices and heat gently. Scoop out the flesh from the apples (it should be soft and frothy) and add this to the pan. Add sugar to taste and serve the drink warm.

JANUARY SONG

The North Wind Doth Blow

The north wind doth blow, and we shall have
   snow,
And what will the robin do then, poor thing?
He'll sit in the barn and keep himself warm,
And hide his head under his wing, poor thing.

END WORD

Ask not the reason, from where it did spring,
For you know very well, it's an old ancient thing.
Cornish song

We cannot really reconnect to the people of the past, who lived their dull, demeaning and laborious lives close to the soil and her seasons. We may live in their houses and drink in the pubs they frequented, but early comers or late, we cannot relive the kinds of feasts and fairs which punctuated their calendar, except in spirit. They were part of the Earth, directly her children working at her tasks. We are largely observers, trying perhaps to reconstruct the patterns under the plough, the magics of seasonal activity, or the harvests in which we have played no part of cultivation. We need those old links, we who are mainly urban children, nurtured in streets, fêted in school yards, entertained by artificial flashing boxes in our living rooms. We don't have the skill to determine the weather prospects from the flight of gnats, or the direction of the wind; we rely on the TV weather person as to the need for a raincoat.

We cannot help the evolution of urban living, but we may regret the loss of our ancestral roots in the soil, connected as cogwheels to the cycling of seasons. In our digitally-watched days, and our neon-lit nights, we have no need for sundials or the light of the stars. But underneath the suburban veneer beats the heart of a child longing to restore the meaning of the pattern of life. Some of us may desire the comfort of the cycle that repeats, the life that returns after barren winter, the life that returns after that imposter, Death, has passed by.

There is no way back, but there is an ancient pathway before us, which, if we can clear away the brambles that clog it, and cut back the trees that overhang it, leads back to the traditional Dancing Grounds, the mazes on the wanton green, the maypoles and the sacred springs, whose water comes to us from the supermarket in plastic bottles!

We can open our hearts to understand the foundations of the ancient celebrations that religious bigotry, civilisation, urbanisation and various acts of parliament have tried to separate us from – it is our heritage, waiting to be reclaimed. We do not have to revert to paganism, or install a Hermit at the bottom of the garden, or invite Druids to take over the local chapel. All we need to do is to recognise the value of the simple, the Creator made, the wild and natural things about us, cherish them, and honour their appearance, season by season, each in their turn, and their disappearance, like the snows of winter, which, who knows, may already have departed from southern England due to mankind's carelessness with the source of life. We are part of the Earth, made of her substance, involved in what happens to the biosphere, the seas, the meadows and the agricultural lands. If we have gone too far already then we are doomed. There may have been a lifeboat at the time of Creation, but if there was, we are already in it, and now it is not so seaworthy in the oceans of space.

If we can learn to reverence what is good, natural or manmade, and hold as valuable those small things in the world, the wild flowers, the trees in such wide variety, the animals, both domestic and wild, so that their lives are as harmonious and natural as can be managed, it will be a step in the right direction. It is not only the Earth that is sacred, our Mother Gaia, but the passing phases, Spring, Summer, Autumn and Winter, and all the gifts they bring unbidden to our lives. We must learn to appreciate these and give them honour. If not, we may be the last generation to have a sacred cycle to wonder at. Humanity is an endangered species too!

BIBLIOGRAPHY

There is a great variety of books on local customs and traditions to be found in public libraries and bookshops. Tourist Boards of different regions will often have leaflets on Seasonal Feasts and local special events.

Alford, V. *The Hobby Horse and Other Animal Masks*, Merlin Press, 1978.

Ball, I. *Traditional Beer and Cider Making*, Paperfronts, 1984.

Carey, D. and Large, J. *Festivals, Family and Food*, Hawthorn Press, 1983.

Edwards, G. *Hogmanay and Tiffany*, Geoffrey Bles, 1970.

Evans, G. Ewart, *The Pattern Under the Plough*, Faber, 1958.

Green, M. *A Harvest of Festivals*, Longmans, 1980.

Green, M.A. *Festive Crafts*, Muller, 1983.

Hoffman, D. *The Holistic Herbal*, Element Books, 1983.

Hole, C. *Dictionary of British Folk Customs*, Granada, 1978.

Hone, M. *Modern Textbook of Astrology*, Foulsham, 1951.

Kightly, C. *The Customs and Ceremonies of Britain*, Thames & Hudson, 1986.

Kightly, C. *The Perpetual Almanack of Folklore*, Thames & Hudson, 1987.

Mann, A.T. *The Round Art*, Paper Tiger, 1979.

Palmer, G. and Lloyd, Noel. *A Year of Festivals*, Warne, 1972.

Strong, R. *The English Year*, Webb & Bower, 1982.

White, F. *Good Things in England*, Futura, 1932.

INDEX